Nuffield
Home Economics
FIBRES AND
FABRICS

General Editor, Nuffield Home Economics
Marie Edwards

Authors of this book
Barbara Booth
John Pomeroy

Contributors to the Background reading
Jeremy Barbour-Hill
David Duke-Williams, Hatra (Hosiery and Allied Trades Research Association)
Ralph Hancock
Philip Jacobs
Frank Kitson
Christine Knowles
D.M. Repper, James H. Heal & Co. Ltd
Pauline Swaine, Lever Brothers Ltd
John Turnpenny
Roger Weston, Ethel Austin & Co. Ltd

Organizers, Nuffield Home Economics 1977—81
Harry Faulkner
Sharon M. Mansell

The Nuffield-Chelsea Curriculum Trust would also like to thank the following for their help:

International Institute for Cotton
International Wool Secretariat
Shirley Institute

Nuffield Home Economics

FIBRES AND FABRICS

Published for the Nuffield-Chelsea Curriculum Trust by Hutchinson Education

Hutchinson & Co. (Publishers) Ltd
An imprint of the Hutchinson Publishing Group
17—21 Conway Street, London W1P 6JD

Hutchinson Group (Australia) Pty Ltd
30—32 Cremorne Street, Richmond South, Victoria 3121
PO Box 151, Broadway, New South Wales 2007

Hutchinson Group (NZ) Ltd
32—34 View Road, PO Box 40—086, Glenfield, Auckland 10

Hutchinson Group (SA) (Pty) Ltd
PO Box 337, Bergvlei 2012, South Africa

First published 1983

© Nuffield-Chelsea Curriculum Trust 1983

British Library Cataloguing in Publication Data
Nuffield-Chelsea Curriculum Trust
    Fibres and fabrics.— (Nuffield home economics)
    Pupils' text
    1. Textile fabrics
    I. Title   II. Series
    677   TS1445

ISBN 0 09 152851 8

Design and art direction by Ivan and Robin Dodd

Printed in Great Britain by The Anchor Press Ltd
and bound by Wm Brendon & Son Ltd
both of Tiptree, Essex

CONTENTS

Acknowledgements

Heather Angel: 4.3a.
Laura Ashley Ltd: 10.5.
Associated Sports Photography: 14.4.
Ethel Austin Ltd: 1.9, 1.10.
Australian Information Service, London: 3.6, 5.6d, e.
BASF: 3.9.
BBC Hulton Picture Library: 6.13.
Courtesy F.H. Barber & Co. Ltd/ Frank Kitson: 2.14.
Barnaby's Picture Library: 2.2c, 2.13c, 3.5, 4.3b, 5.6a, c, 5.7, 12.8, 12.10, 13.1.
British Aerospace, Aircraft Group, Weybridge-Bristol Division: 2.1d.
British Fur Trade Association: 3.8a.
British Wool Marketing Board: 5.11.
Bob Bray: 8.3b, 11.6.
Paul Brierley: 14.5.
Canadian High Commission: 3.10b.
J. Allan Cash Ltd: 2.1c, 2.2b, d, 3.8b, 4.5a, b, 4.9, 12.7.
Chelsea College, Audio Visual Service Unit: 2.3, 2.5a, b, c, 2.7, 2.8, 3.11, 7.2, 7.6c, 7.14, 7.16a, 9.8, 13.3, 13.10, 13.12, 13.13.
J. & P. Coats Ltd: 13.17.
R.J. Corbin: 10.2.
Courtaulds Ltd: 1.6c, 2.13a, 4.1, 6.9, 7.16b, 9.12, 9.13, 11.1b, 11.7, 11.9.
Ministry of Defence: 1.6d.
Dunlop Ltd: 7.15.
E.I. du Pont de Nemours & Co: 4.7.
Electricity Council, Understanding Electricity: 8.3a, 15.11, 15.12, 15.13.
Department of the Environment. Crown copyright. Reproduced by permission of the Controller, H.M.S.O: 5.5.
Mary Evans Picture Library: 2.1b, 8.3a.
Ford Photographic Services: 1.6b, 2.1a, 13.4.
Forestry Commission: 3.10a.
John Godrich: 12.11.
Harrods Ltd: 2.11a.
James H. Heal & Co. Ltd: 7.19, 7.20.
Adrian Hewitt: 3.13.
Home Laundering Consultative Council: table 15.1.
Hosiery and Allied Trades Research Association (HATRA): 8.10, 13.14.
Houseman Burnham Ltd: 15.8.
Imperial Chemical Industries plc, Fibres Division: 2.13b, 3.2a, b, 4.4.
Inner London Education Authority, Learning Materials Service: 1.4.
International Institute for Cotton: 5.1, 5.2a, b, c, 5.3a, b, c, 13.18.

International Wool Secretariat: 5.4, 5.6b, 7.8, 9.11, 11.5, 12.1, 12.2, 12.6, 12.12, 13.7.
Philip Jacobs: 11.10, 11.11.
Jean Machine: 2.2a.
Frank Kitson: 1.1, 1.6e, f, g, h, 2.11b, c, d, 3.10d, 7.4, 7.6a, b, 7.13, 11.4, 14.3a, 15.1, 15.2, 15.9a.
Janusz Konrad: 1.8.
Textile Physics Laboratory, University of Leeds: 2.9.
LAT Photographic: 14.2.
Mansell Collection Ltd: 2.6, 2.15, 3.3, 4.10, 9.3, 14.1, 15.10.
Mossley Wool Combing & Spinning Co. Ltd: 8.3c.
Mothercare plc: 1.6a.
Professor Denis Munden: 13.16.
National Water Council: 15.6, 15.7.
Nature Photographers Ltd: 4.3c.
High Commissioner for New Zealand: 9.2.
Oxford Scientific Films/G.I. Bernard: 4.2d, 5.9a, b, c, d.
Pegg-Whiteley Ltd: 11.1a.
Presseagentur/Sven Simon: 3.10c.
Ann Ronan Picture Library: 15.9b.
W. Schlafhorst & Co: 9.9.
Science Museum, London: 6.1, 9.19.
Shirley Institute: 1.7, 6.2, 6.3, 6.5, 6.12, 7.18, 8.5a, b, 8.6, 9.10, 9.18, 11.3, 13.6, 13.15a, b.
Silk Educational Service: 5.8.
Style Patterns Ltd: 13.5.
Tootal Group plc: 12.3.
Topham Picture Library: 3.7, 4.2a, b, c.
Unilever Magazine: 15.14.
Unilever Research: 14.3b, 15.3, 15.4, 15.5.

Illustrations by Robin Dodd, Rodney Paull, Christine Roche, Gary Simmons, and Ian Smith.

Tables by Nina Konrad.

Introduction

What are you looking for when you go shopping for clothes?
Do you want to buy something in particular? Are you looking
for something attractive, something that will last a long time,
something that doesn't cost too much, or a combination of all
three? This book will help you to make sensible choices and to
avoid expensive mistakes.

In *Fibres and fabrics* you will learn about the textiles you and
your family buy, wear, and see about you. Why do your wear
textiles rather than sheets of plastic? How are man-made fibres
made? What are the differences between clothes made of man-
made fibres and natural fibres? What are the advantages and
disadvantages of each? Why are so many fabrics made of a
mixture of different fibres? What effect does the structure of a
fabric have on its properties? What is 'finishing'? How are
dyeing and printing done, and what are their effects? These are
some of the questions you will consider in *Fibres and fabrics*.
There are plenty of experiments and other practical work to
help you learn to observe things carefully, to classify them,
and to suggest reasons for what you see.

CHAPTER 1
Going shopping

1.1
HOW DO YOU CHOOSE?

Think of the last time you went shopping for clothes, or for anything made out of fabric. Perhaps you looked for something you needed or perhaps you just felt like buying something. What you bought could have been expensive or cheap. What was it?

Q 1

Write down what you bought. List as many reasons as you can think of for why you bought that particular item, and not, for example, another coat on the same rail. Put down every reason, however small. Did you like the buttons, for example?

Your list may include some of these reasons, and others: attractive colour; washable; cheap; well made; different; wanted something special; in the sale; went with my hair; matched the wallpaper; went with some clothes I already had; like all my friends were wearing; makes me look grown up; my girlfriend liked it; I thought it would last a long time; keep me warm in winter.

You might have given some of these reasons or you may have different ones. One thing is certain, throughout the class there will be many different reasons.

UNDERSTANDING THE CHOICE

You will have put down all sorts of reasons, but you will find that they can be sorted into three groups, that is, you can classify them.

Figure 1.1
Choosing an item of clothing.

Figure 1.2

1432   1632

2

Figure 1.4

1952   1982

1 Reasons to do with fashion or the impression that the garment (whatever it was) gives. A name for these reasons is *aesthetic factors*. 'Aesthetic' means roughly, 'having to do with our feelings about it'.

2 Reasons to do with how an item behaves over a period of time: how well it wears, how easy it is to clean, and so on. Call these *performance factors*.

3 Reasons to do with money. These are *price factors*.

Q 2
Classify the reasons suggested at the beginning of this section into the three groups as in figure 1.3.

Aesthetics	Performance	Price
attractive colour	washable	cheap

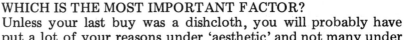

Figure 1.3

Q 3
Now do the same for your own list.

WHICH IS THE MOST IMPORTANT FACTOR?
Unless your last buy was a dishcloth, you will probably have put a lot of your reasons under 'aesthetic' and not many under 'performance'. But even if all you want of something is that it should 'look good' it has to have some standard of performance. Even a wedding dress that is worn only once has to last through the wedding!

Most things have to be worn more than once and so will need cleaning. You might not consciously think of this when you buy something, but some thought of performance is quite often at the back of your mind. For example, you might avoid a shop that sells clothes which tend to fall apart even though they are cheap. Which factor is most important — aesthetic, performance, or price — or does it vary?

ORDER OF IMPORTANCE

Q 4
What was the order of importance of the factors for the item you bought?

For most of you it will probably be aesthetics first followed by price. Now, suppose you were buying something different, for example a pair of trousers for a young schoolboy (figure 1.4). What would be the order then?

It is almost certain that performance or price will have come first and aesthetics last. So you can see that the importance of

3

the factors can vary from item to item. You can also say that the same person will have different requirements for different garments. Can it also vary from person to person?

Q 5
Suppose a very rich and a very poor person went shopping for a winter coat. What would their order of priorities be?

Figure 1.5

RATING THE FACTORS

As you have seen, the factors can be put into an order of importance for a particular item. But is it enough just to put them in order?

Suppose you are buying a handkerchief as a Christmas present. You will look for a nice design and colour (aesthetics). Perhaps you will check that the colours will not fade or run in the wash (performance). But say you have budgeted to spend 50p on that present. Then the price will be by far the most important factor. It will outweigh the others in any decision.

How can you rate the relative importance of each factor? You could use a scale from 1 to 10, where 10 is the highest rating. For the handkerchief, price would rate 10 and aesthetics might rate 5 or 6 (if you were looking for a nice design). Performance would probably rate lower, perhaps 3. If performance had been almost completely unimportant it would have rated 1.

Figure 1.6

Q 6

How would you rate the three factors for the articles shown on these two pages?

Q 7

This information is easier to understand on a bar chart. Draw an example of a bar chart using your ratings for five of the items shown in figure 1.6.

HOW DO YOU DECIDE WHAT TO CHOOSE?

‖ YOU WILL NEED: ‖‖

Pictures of various garments

Look at the pictures and select items which will make up an outfit you would like to wear.

Q 8

Rate the factors for each item as you did in question 6. Compare your choice and ratings with those made by others in the class.

What you choose and the way you rate any item is mostly personal. Clothes are often used as a reflection of your personality: how you see yourself, or how you wish others to see you.

1.2
CONSUMERS AND SUPPLIERS

Whenever you buy something you are a customer or a *consumer*. You, the consumer, make a choice and rate the factors in order of importance — even if you do not do it in the exact way described here. The people selling the items have also rated the factors. If they have got the balance of factors correct, they will fit your needs and you will buy the item. Successful suppliers get the balance right for the largest number of people. Unsuccessful ones fail to sell and go out of business.

1.3
WHERE DOES SCIENCE COME IN?

Scientists study materials of all kinds. They put forward and test ideas to explain how materials react in different ways and in different circumstances. The tests are models of what the materials will have to stand up to in real life. They allow scientists to predict how the materials will perform under various conditions.

Tests on textiles show how they behave when you wear or use them and when they are washed or dry cleaned. Changing the way a textile is made, or the raw material it is made of, changes its performance. This change may or may not be an improvement. The performance of a textile is measured and rated so that different materials can be compared. If the performance of a material is poor, further tests can be devised to show why.

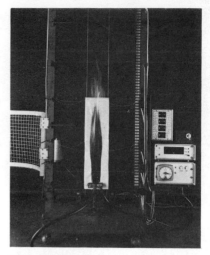

Figure 1.7
A flammability test.

SCIENCE AND TECHNOLOGY
With this knowledge a *technology* is built up which allows manufacturers to make materials that will give the required standard of performance. Technology is the scientific study of industrial and mechanical ways of making things.

Q 9
List some of the performance requirements for a shirt or blouse.

SCIENCE AND AESTHETICS
Science influences performance; but can it influence aesthetic factors?

Q 10
List some of your aesthetic requirements for a shirt or blouse.

Aesthetic factors are a matter of your own choice — but science and technology can affect them. Suppose you want a polyester blouse in a particular colour. The manufacturer who rightly guesses that you will want that colour has to choose a dye which will give that colour on polyester. The dye chosen must not fade or run when you wash the blouse. He needs a knowledge of technology to choose the right dye.

Q 11
List two other performance properties which could be affected by aesthetic requirements.

SCIENCE AND PRICE
The price you can afford to pay is clearly related to how much money you have. It is nothing to do with science. But technical factors do affect cost. For example, certain colours on polyester may be difficult to obtain and special dyeing methods must be used. The colour you want for your blouse might need a very expensive dye, so that blouse will be more expensive than the same style in another colour. Whether you choose to pay extra for the colour is up to you, but at least science can show you *why* the price is higher.

Figure 1.8
Roger Weston.

Figure 1.9

1.4
COMPROMISES

For these reasons there is usually a compromise between the properties of textile items and your choice. You might get the right aesthetics at the right price but with a poor performance. If the performance and price are right you might not like the look of the garment. As a consumer, of course, you want all three factors to be perfect. But in practice you have to settle for a compromise. Science cannot make the choice for you. However, it can help you to understand performance and how this ties in with aesthetics and price. Knowing this you can make the most appropriate choice.

BACKGROUND READING

THE BUYER

Before you buy a T-shirt, a pair of socks, or any other item of clothing, someone employed by the shop will have chosen and bought it from a supplier. This is the job of the buyer. Roger Weston is a buyer for the Ethel Austin chain of shops. They have over seventy shops in the north-west of England and in north Wales selling ladies' and children's clothing. Roger Weston's job is to decide what will sell and to make sure that Ethel Austin shops are supplied.

Clothes are often ordered by the buyer six or nine months before they are sold in the shops. So, the first thing Roger considers is the season he is buying for. He knows that you will want light and colourful clothes in summer and heavy and warm clothes in the winter. If it is spring when you are reading this, Roger is probably discussing the clothes that you will be wearing next winter.

Design and colour are the next major considerations. Roger knows that the way a garment looks is very important to you.

Figure 1.10

To help him choose, he has to think about what was fashionable last year; what the top designers are doing; and what people are buying in other countries.

A great deal of thought goes into establishing what the customer will want. But no one can foresee the future: does this mean that a part of the buyer's decision is guesswork? Roger says no. A buyer should *never* just guess. He explains that although he places orders some months in advance of a season, if he is unsure of a particular style he will only buy a small quantity. This is put into the shops to let the customer decide whether she wants it or not. In cases like this, the buyer must make sure that his suppliers can respond quickly to repeat orders.

As the buyer decides what will be available in the shops, does this mean that the buyer is telling you what to buy? Again Roger disagrees. Customers buy some lines and leave others on the rails. If the buyer does not buy what the customer wants, Roger can tell because he sees full rails of clothes. If he gets it right, the rails empty and he orders more. And, as Roger points out, the customer can always go to another company's shops.

Roger feels that communication is the key to success in his job. He must constantly assess information received from suppliers, manufacturers, trade shows, magazines, competitor's shops, and, most of all, from his customers. He cannot tell the true reaction to his merchandise just from figures. The buyer must sometimes get out into the 'field' and talk to shop assistants who are in closest touch with the most important person — you.

CHAPTER 2
The clothes line

Figure 2.1

2.1
THE VARIETY OF TEXTILES

Everyone realizes that clothes are made of textiles, but have you ever thought of all the things in your house and in your neighbourhood that are also made from textiles?

Q 1

Look at the photographs on this page. They show scenes which are probably quite familiar to you. In these scenes textiles are being used in a variety of ways. Make a list of as many uses of textiles as you can find or think of in each photograph.

You will find a great number of uses of textiles in figure 2.1. This is why the textile industry is so large. Because textiles have so many uses, this book will concentrate just on clothing and some household textile articles. There are, of course, many types of clothing.

Q 2

Make a list of as many different garments that are in everyday use as you can think of.

The clothes you wear depend on custom, social factors, and the climate in the part of the World you live in.

Figure 2.2a
Typical Western clothing.

Figure 2.2b
Traditional Arab clothing.

Figure 2.2d
Traditional Eskimo clothing.

Figure 2.2c
African tribesmen.

The study of how people live, what they wear, and their traditions and customs is called *social anthropology*. This book is mainly concerned with the everyday garments worn by people in Western society. (Worksheet FM2 has more information on textiles in your home.)

2.2
BREAKING DOWN A GARMENT: STAGE ONE
If you take a garment apart you will see all the separate parts which go to make it. Look at figure 2.3. There is a main body fabric (and there may be several pieces of this) and the trimmings. There will be a variety of trimmings.

Q 3
How many different sorts of trimmings can you think of? Make a list of them.

2.3
LOOKING AT SOME OF THE PARTS
The main body fabric is obviously the most important part of a garment. You can find out something about it by doing the tests in the rest of the chapter.

HANDLING TESTS
What does the fabric feel like?

|||| YOU WILL NEED: |||||||||||||||||||||||||||||||||||||||||||||||
Part of a main body fabric

1 Examine the fabric in your hands in the way shown in figure 2.4.

Q 4
Now describe a property of your fabric.

You might have said that your fabric was soft or harsh, smooth or knobbly. You might have found it difficult to describe the actual feel or *handle* of the fabric. You might have described the way the fabric hangs or *drapes* instead.

2 Lay your fabric over your arm and then over your knee.

Q 5
After these tests, how would you describe the properties of your fabric?

From these simple handling tests you might have used words like 'floppy', 'pliable', or 'hangs easily' to describe the fabric. Again, it might have been difficult to find the right words. This is because you are trying to describe another aesthetic factor.

One property of all textiles is that they will drape and mould to the shape of your body. However, you have also found out that textiles can easily be moved out of shape (*distorted*) but that they will easily return to their original shape. Think of what happens to a jacket sleeve when you bend and unbend your arm. This makes textiles comfortable to wear.

Figure 2.4

Figure 2.3
A man's jacket dissected.

collar 'canvas' or interlining

labels

pocketing

main fabric

interlining

hanging loop

lining

sewing thread

shoulder pad

sleeve lining

11

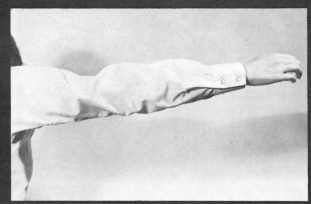

Figure 2.5a

Figure 2.5b

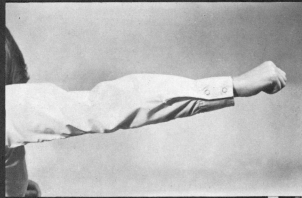

Figure 2.5c

Figure 2.6
Just think what it would be like to wear a suit of armour all day!

Handling a fabric has told you something about its aesthetic properties, but has it told you anything about its performance and price?

You won't be able to tell how much a fabric costs just from handling it. However, an expert would be able to make a guess at the price from the aesthetic factors, as these factors affect the price.

Handling alone will not tell you what the performance of a fabric will be. To do this you will need to know what the fabric is made from and look in more detail at how it has been put together.

2.4
BREAKING DOWN A GARMENT: STAGE TWO

What is the fabric made of? This stage involves the dissection of the main body of the garment.

|||| YOU WILL NEED: ||||||||||||||||||||||||||||||||||||||||||||||||||||||||||||||||||||||||||||||||||||||
Main body fabric   Hand lens
                                    Instrument for dissecting

Using the instrument you have been given, take apart some of the main body fabric. You may need the hand lens to see what you are doing.

Having started with a flat fabric, you should now have a pile of long yarns. Some of the yarns may be thicker than others but they will all be fairly thin. If you pick up a pile of yarns it will easily fall apart. It is easy to see why.

In a fabric the yarns do not easily fall apart because they are arranged in a special way, that is, they are *interlaced*. In the pile, the yarns are just jumbled together.

Figure 2.7
Pull out some threads of main body fabric into a pile.

Figure 2.8
A yarn with one end dissected.

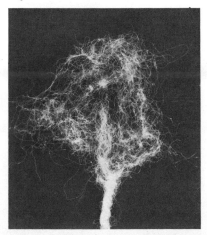

Q 6
Draw a diagram or picture of the way the yarns in your fabric are interlaced. You will probably find it useful to use the hand lens to see the interlacing clearly.

There are two main ways of interlacing yarns. These are *weaving* and *knitting*.

2.5
BREAKING DOWN A GARMENT: STAGE THREE

What are the yarns like? What are they made of?

|||| YOU WILL NEED: ||||||||||||||||||||||||||||||||||||||||||||||||||||||||||||||||||||||||||||
Yarns taken from main body fabric   Fine dissecting needle
                                     Powerful hand lens

1 Take a yarn from the main body fabric.

2 Take the yarn apart using the fine dissecting needle and a powerful hand lens.

You may find this fiddly to do. It is sometimes easier if you twist the yarn between your thumb and forefinger, as this can help to open up the yarn. However you do it, you will start with a long thin yarn and end up with a pile of much finer *fibres*.

EXAMINING THE FIBRES
What are the fibres like?

|||| YOU WILL NEED: ||||||||||||||||||||||||||||||||||||||||||||||||||||||||||||||||||||||||||||||||||||||

Fibres taken from sample yarn

Fine dissecting needle
Powerful hand lens
Microscope

1 Look carefully at the length of your fibres using your hand lens.

Usually the fibres will be much shorter than the yarn you started with, but sometimes the fibre can be as long as the yarn. Either way you have reached the raw material of textiles — the fibre.

2 Now look at some of your fibres under the microscope.

Can you pull the fibres apart to make them any smaller?

You could cut the fibres to make them smaller, but you could not take them apart as you did with the fabric and the yarn. The fibre is a chemical compound. It is made up of smaller parts: each part is a *molecule* of the fibre. There are millions of molecules in the smallest piece of fibre you may have. They are far too small to be seen by the eye or even the most powerful optical microscope. Special instruments are needed to look at the molecules of a fibre (see figure 2.9).

2.6
STAGE REVIEW

Q 7
Draw a chart to show how a garment can be taken apart step by step.

Your chart should be a chain — that is, each step leads on to the next. The chain shows the breakdown of the garment into smaller and smaller parts or *components*. If you reverse the chain you can see how the garment is built up from its smallest components.

2.7
THE CHAIN OF TRADE
A name for this chain might be 'the clothes line'. It shows the line of processes needed to make clothes. You could also call it the 'chain of trade'. Each stage in the chain represents a section of trade or industry which is responsible for making the clothes you wear.

The first stage corresponds to the fibre manufacturer. In natural fibres the molecules are produced by a growing plant or animal.

14

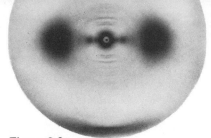

Figure 2.9
X-ray diffraction photograph of a wool fibre.

Figure 2.11a
Department store.

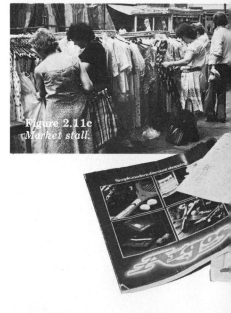

Figure 2.11c
Market stall.

They are collected by the grower as fibres. For man-made fibres the molecules are made in a chemical factory and produced in fibre form.

The second stage in the chain is the yarn producer or spinner who makes the fibres into yarns.

The third stage is the fabric producer who may be a weaver or knitter. The fabric producer changes the yarn into fabric. Stages two and three are often linked together and called the 'textile trade'.

Figure 2.11b
Chain store.

The fourth stage, changing a fabric into a garment, is the job of the clothier or garment manufacturer. This is carried out by a tailor or dressmaker or someone known by the name connected with a particular garment. For example, someone who makes hats is called a milliner. They form what is called the clothing trade or industry, sometimes jokingly known as 'the rag trade'.

Figure 2.10
The chain of trade.

Figure 2.11d
Mail order

Q 8
Now draw a complete chain showing where you (the consumer) will be.

You probably cannot buy clothes or textiles straight from the factory. Most clothes are bought from a *retailer*. This is a person (or firm) who buys clothes from a number of factories and then sells them to the public. This can be done in many ways.

Q 9
Make a list of as many ways of 'retailing' as you can think of. The photographs in figure 2.11 may help you.

So the chain of trade should be extended to include retailers, with you, the consumer, at the end.

Figure 2.12
The complete chain of trade.

Although this book is concerned mainly with clothing, there are many other textile items. Household textiles, such as chair covers, sheets, and towels are all made of fabric. Therefore, they also follow the chain of trade — except that the clothier would just be known as a maker up. This is an important area of textiles and, like clothing, it has definite fashion trends (figure 2.13).

For some of the other areas of the textile industry the chain of trade must be altered. Two of these areas are piece goods (fabric you buy to do your own home garment making) and carpets.

Figure 2.13
a *Modern bed with continental quilt, fitted sheet, and valance.*
b *Divan bed.*
c *Four-poster bed with curtains.*

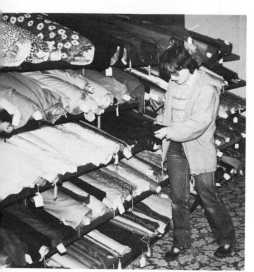

Figure 2.14
Fabrics (piece goods) for sale in a department store.

Figure 2.15
Eli Whitney's cotton gin. The wire teeth on the drum strip the hairs from the seeds.

Q 10
Draw a new diagram of the chain for piece goods and carpets.

BACKGROUND READING

KING COTTON

Cotton is much the most important of all textile fibres, making up nearly half the World's total fibre production. There are many reasons for this, and far-reaching consequences.

Cotton is popular because it is generally cheap. The cloth is easily dyed and makes comfortable clothes because it absorbs moisture. Most cotton cloth is washable. The best grades of cotton with long fibres, such as West Indian sea island cotton, make fine, almost silky cloth. For the grower, cotton is a profitable crop. It grows in warm climates and resists drought.

As a result, cotton is grown in about 80 countries which in all produce 15 million tonnes a year. The main producers are China, the Soviet Union, and the United States. However, in many Third World countries in Africa and tropical America cotton is vitally important. For example Sudan depends almost entirely on cotton exports for its foreign earnings. Some countries earn much money by processing cotton or making cotton clothing, for example Hong Kong.

A decline in the cotton industry can be disastrous. Until a few decades ago a huge amount of cotton cloth was woven in Lancashire, much of it for export. The industry was nicknamed 'King Cotton' because of its influence in the region. Now the same goods can be made more cheaply in Third World countries — good news for them but bad news for Lancashire, where the industry is in a severe slump.

Cotton comes from a small, bushy plant which is related to okra (bhindi, gumbo). Instead of being edible, its pods — called bolls — contain seeds surrounded by hairs 1 to 3 cm long. These hairs are the cotton fibres. When they are separated from the seeds, the seeds are pressed to give cooking oil and their crushed remains made into cattle feed. These by-products make extra money for producers and also mean that the cotton plant is a very important source of foodstuffs.

Cotton plants originally grew wild both in Asia and in tropical America. Cotton clothing has been made in India since prehistoric times. Europeans discovered cotton in the fourth century B.C. when Alexander the Great's army invaded India. After this the plant was introduced to Egypt and Greece. The American cotton plant was also used early, but white settlers found that in this type the hairs were difficult to pull off the seeds. In 1793 Eli Whitney invented the cotton gin (short for engine) with a revolving drum studded with wire hooks. It did the job quickly and well. The American cotton industry grew enormously, thanks to slave labour. It was to free the slaves in the southern states that the Civil War was fought in the 1860s.

CHAPTER 3

Why textiles
– why not plastics?

3.1
WHY SO MANY PROCESSES?

Think back to the clothes line from raw material to finished garment that you saw in Chapter 2.

Figure 3.1

From looking at figure 3.1 you might think there are only two processing steps needed to make a garment, but you would be wrong. Many more processing steps are needed to produce a textile fabric. To start with, a yarn must be produced from the fibres. The yarn must then be made into a fabric. Even then the process is not complete; before the fabric can be sent to a garment manufacturer it must be *finished*. This means that a number of processes have to be carried out on the fabric. Some of these are simple, such as washing, and some are far more complicated. You will find out more about this in Chapter 12.

Q 1
Copy figure 3.1 into your book, but change it to show all the processes from fibre to finished garment.

Q 2
How many processing steps are there?

Each processing step needs different machines to carry it out. Therefore, each extra processing step costs money. Machines are not the only things which add to the cost of more processing steps.

Q 3
What other things add to the cost of each new processing step? (Figure ? may give you some clues.)

Figure 3.2a

Figure 3.2b

As you can see, making textiles is expensive because of the number of processes. So why not use something else? What you are looking for is a two-dimensional material, like fabric, which can be made into a three-dimensional shape, like a garment, but using simpler methods.

3.2
SKINS AND FURS

Nobody really knows when textile fabrics were first made. Some pieces of cloth have been found in Swiss lake dwellings dating from around 6500 B.C. However, it is certain that before this Man relied on skins and furs for clothing. This is known because stone tools used to scrape the skins have been found.

An animal skin is a two-dimensional material. When an animal is killed, the skin is removed and with it comes any hair or fur. A lot of cleaning is needed to remove the flesh (hence the prehistoric scrapers) but even then the skin is still hard and stiff and needs softening. Primitive Man did this by beating. It can also be done by chewing.

Nowadays machinery and chemicals are used to soften skins but it still means there are several processes involved, and these cost money. This is one of the reasons why garments made from skins or furs are expensive. Have you been to a shop or looked at a mail-order catalogue, and compared the cost of a real fur or leather coat with the prices of those made from a textile fabric? On average the coats made from textiles will be much cheaper.

There are other cost problems involved in using animal skins and furs. Some of the skins which have a high aesthetic value come from animals which have to be hunted — which is expensive. Many of these animals are now rare and are protected species.

Figure 3.3
Swiss lake dwellings.

Figure 3.4
Cleaning skins.

Figure 3.5
Leopard.

Figure 3.6
Shearing sheep.

Figure 3.7
Mink.

Figure 3.8a

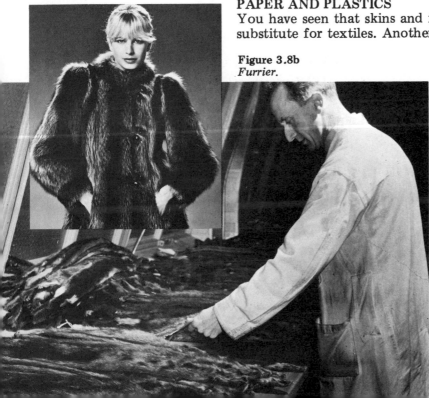

Some skins and furs come from domesticated or farm animals. However, sheep or cows take a long time to grow and have to be kept and fed. This costs money. Have you ever thought why a sheepskin coat is generally more expensive than a coat made from a wool textile fabric — even though there may have been a lot of extra making up in the textile coat? The reason is that to make a woollen coat you need wool which is obtained by shearing sheep. The wool on the sheep then grows again.

To get a sheepskin coat you need to kill the sheep. It takes more than one sheep's skin to make a sheepskin coat. One animal whose skin is used for clothes and is especially bred for the purpose is the mink. But the mink is quite a small animal.

Q 4
How many minks do you think it would take to make a full-length fur coat?

All the skins have to be sewn together to make the coat by the furrier. This is a time-consuming and expensive process.

Cost, however, is not the only reason why skins and furs are not everyday clothing items. Have you ever tried wearing a fur coat or leather jacket on a hot or even a warm day? They are uncomfortably hot. For most people high cost and lack of comfort make skins and furs of limited appeal.

Q 5
For which group of people are skin and fur clothing most suitable? Why?

3.3
PAPER AND PLASTICS
You have seen that skins and furs are generally impractical as a substitute for textiles. Another alternative might be plastics.

Figure 3.8b
Furrier.

Figure 3.9
Polythene sheet extrusion.

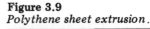

A sheet of plastic, such as polythene, is made very simply from the basic material (polythene chips) in one process.

Q 6
Which is likely to be more expensive — textile fabric or a sheet of plastic?

Another cheap method of making a two-dimensional material is the paper-making process. If you think about the great variety of paper items in use you will realize how cheap paper must be.

Q 7
How many jackets could you make from a Sunday newspaper?

Paper and plastics are two reasonably cheap materials. They are certainly cheaper than textile fabrics, so why not use them to make clothes? To answer that question, go back to the three factors determining choice — aesthetics, performance, and price. Paper and plastic have a price advantage over textiles, but what about their aesthetics and performance?

MAKING GARMENTS FROM DIFFERENT MATERIALS

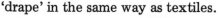

IIII YOU WILL NEED: IIIIIIIIIIIIIIIIIIIIIIIIIIIIIIIIIIIIIIIIIIIIIIIIIIIIIIIIIIIIIIIIIIIIIIIIIIIIIIIIIIIIII

Paper, plastic, and textile fabric pieces (cut into shape)	Scissors
	Pins
Thread	Sewing machine

1 Construct a simple garment or section of a garment from paper, plastic, and a textile fabric (see figure 3.11).

2 Compare the aesthetics of the garments you have made (as you did in Chapter 2).

3 If necessary wear the garments to help you compare them.

3.4
LOOKING AT THE PROBLEMS
As you found earlier, it is always difficult to describe aesthetic factors. For use as clothing, paper and plastics do not seem to have the right 'handle'. You must have noticed that they do not 'drape' in the same way as textiles.

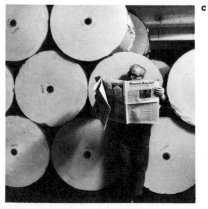

Figure 3.10
Paper:
a *trees.*
b *paper mill.*
c *paper sheet.*
d *uses of paper.*

Figure 3.11a
Skirt made from paper.

Figure 3.11b
Skirt made from plastic.

Figure 3.11c
Skirt made from a textile fabric.

Q 8

How do you think this will affect their comfort in wear? (Think back to the knight in his suit of armour in Chapter 2.)

Apart from aesthetics, you must also think of performance. The tear strength of a material is an important performance factor.

TEAR STRENGTHS OF MATERIALS

|||| YOU WILL NEED: |||||||||||||||||||||||||||||||||||||||||||||||||||||||||||||||||||||||||||||

Piece of plastic, 10 cm × 10 cm
Piece of paper, 10 cm × 10 cm
Piece of fabric, 10 cm × 10 cm
Whatever else you think necessary

How would you set up an experiment to compare the strengths of the three materials?

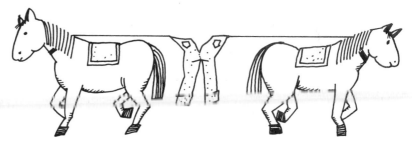

Figure 3.12

Some of the materials you have been looking at lack strength as well as not being aesthetically pleasing. (Worksheet FM8 is about the strengths of fibres used in woven fabrics.)

You will have found that for materials of similar thickness, the textile fabric is the strongest. Paper clearly does not have enough strength for ordinary wear. Plastic is not really strong enough unless it is very thick. The thicker the plastic is made, the stiffer it becomes. This makes it even more unacceptable aesthetically. Plastics are used in clothing, but nearly always as a coating on a textile fabric (as in the so-called 'plastic mac').

3.5
WHY ARE TEXTILES BETTER?

You can now see that although paper and plastics are cheap, textile fabrics score on aesthetic and performance factors. (You know from Chapter 1 that the most important factor for clothing is aesthetics.) To find out why, you must look at the starting point for all three materials. The wood pulp used to make paper and the plastic chips used for making plastic sheet do not have the aesthetic qualities needed for the finished materials, but the textile fibres do.

Think back to the textile fibres obtained in section 2.5. These have the right 'handle' and can bend, giving the required draping characteristics. The method of building up a textile fabric — making the yarn and then interlacing the yarn to give the fabric — means that these properties are retained and other properties such as strength are built up.

BACKGROUND READING

WHY NOT PLASTIC — FOR HATS?

Christine Knowles makes hats and jewellery — out of plastic. Plastic as a material for clothing and jewellery has rather a bad reputation. Christine thinks that this is a pity. Because they are made of plastic, her hats and jewellery can be made cheaply, but they are well made, can look very attractive, and fulfil the purpose for which they have been designed.

Christine comes from Carlisle, in Cumbria. She took a four-year course in jewellery at Middlesex Polytechnic. During her course she decided that the material she wanted to work with was plastic and that she wanted to make geometric shapes with it. She then found herself having to learn about the science and technology of her chosen material and about maths and geometry. It was then that she remembered sitting at the back of maths and science lessons at school drawing!

All Christine's hats start off as a sketch of the shape she wants. The sketch is then redrawn very carefully as a technical drawing which is used as a pattern for each piece of the hat. The materials she uses are industrial plastics made by ICI. She has to find out how each plastic will react to being cut, bent, dyed, stuck, and sometimes even sewn. If a plastic will not go into the shape she wants, she either changes the type of plastic used or finds a different way of forming the shape. Gradually, she is building up a *technology* (a way of making things) for plastics used for jewellery and hats.

Christine thinks that too often science and technology are not properly applied to art. When an artist fully understands the science behind the materials he or she is working with, the result is a better painting or sculpture, or, in Christine's case, a better plastic hat.

Figure 3.13

Figure 4.1 (right)
Magnified photograph of the cross-section of polyester fibres.

Figure 4.2 (below)
Some sources of fibres:
a camel b Angora rabbit
c palm tree d silkworm.

CHAPTER 4
Fibres:
the first step in the line

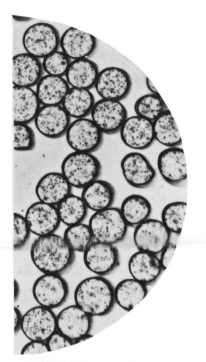

4.1
MANY ARE KNOWN — FEW ARE CHOSEN

You have already seen that fibres are the raw material from which fabrics are made. There are lots of different fibres. Fibres have a particular, recognizable shape. They are very fine, hair-like materials. A mathematical way of saying this is that they are materials which have a length many times greater than their cross-sectional width.

In figure 4.1, the cross-section is almost a circle. Other fibres have a different cross-section from this. Nevertheless, the cross-section is always many times smaller than the length. Fibres come from natural sources, that is, plants and animals, or they can be man-made.

Q 1
In the following list, which ones are fibres? Which of the fibres are man-made?

Aramid, modacrylic, Azlon, kapok, Saran, urena, pineapple, coir, guanaco, vicuna.

Although many fibres are known, in practice only a few are used to make clothing and textile items. Why is this?

Figure 4.3a
Cotton boll.

Figure 4.3b
Sheep.

Figure 4.3c
Silk cocoons.

All fibres are similar in their properties, but there are variations and these are important. Sisal has a rough 'handle', alginate (made from seaweed) dissolves in water, and vicuna is incredibly expensive. Very few fibres are used on a large scale for clothing. This is because only a few provide a satisfactory balance of the three factors — aesthetics, performance, and price. The most popular fibres are those which give the best combination of the three factors for the most garments. (You could use worksheet FM3 to examine different fibres under a microscope.)

Q 2
Name five garments or textile items and the fibre most associated with them. (For example, cotton is associated with handkerchiefs.)

As there are so many different fibres, they must be classified to make it easier to understand the relationship between them. The first main division can be between natural and man-made fibres. You can further divide natural fibres into those which come from plants and those which come from animals. The most important plant fibre is cotton, and the most important animal fibre is wool. However, another animal fibre, silk, must also be considered.

In the past, another plant fibre, linen, was used for clothing but its use has decreased in recent years except for household items.

You can also divide man-made fibres into two types. First, there are those, like viscose, acetate, and triacetate, which are made from natural materials and are called *regenerated* fibres. Secondly, fibres like nylon, polyester, and acrylic are built up from simple chemicals and are called *synthetic* fibres.

Even though fibres are divided into natural and man-made, they are all chemical compounds and they all differ from one another.

Q 3
Draw a classification table showing the important fibres under each heading.

4.2
GENERICS AND OTHERS
When you classified the fibres in question 3, you grouped them according to where they come from. The names you used for the fibres were their general or *generic* names. You may have seen other names for these fibres, particularly the man-made ones — Terylene and Courtelle are examples. This is because manufactured fibres are usually made by more than one company. Sometimes a company will give its own particular product a special, or *brand*, name. Terylene is the brand name of the polyester fibre manufactured by ICI, the large British chemical company. Courtelle is the brand name for the acrylic fibre manufactured by Courtaulds, a large British fibre and textile company.

It is important that you understand the difference between a brand name and a generic name. The generic name tells you the type of fibre used; the brand name tells you who made it. To help you distinguish between generic and brand names, always write the generic name with a small first letter (except at the beginning of a sentence) and the brand name with a capital letter.

WHY USE BRAND NAMES?

Terylene is the brand name for the polyester fibre made by ICI, but polyester is made by many other companies throughout the World. Some companies do not bother to give their product a brand name, but others do.

Q 4
List as many names for polyester fibre as you can, the names of the companies which make them, and the country where they are made.

Of course polyester is not the only fibre with a lot of brand names. All man-made fibres are made by a number of manufacturers who often give their product its own distinctive name. A few of these are shown in table 4.1. Many companies sell their fibres all over the World. Some of them make the same fibre in more than one country.

Generic name	Brand name
viscose	Sarille, Fibro
acetate	Dicel
triacetate	Tricel, Arnel
nylon	Bri-nylon, Blue C, Perlon
acrylic	Courtelle, Acrilan, Orlon, Vonnel

Table 4.1

Q 5
Why should a fibre company go to the expense of building factories to make the same fibre in different parts of the World?

Fibre manufacturers will not allow anyone else to use their brand names. A lot of money is spent on advertising brand names.

Q 6
Why do you think fibre manufacturers give brand names to fibres?

Recently, the generic names for fibres have become more widely known, *e.g.* polyester/cotton fabrics. In Europe, the regulations of the European Economic Community (the E.E.C.) demand that all garments have the generic names of the fibres they are made from clearly visible to the consumer in the shop.

Q 7
Why do you think the E.E.C. Commission insists on this?

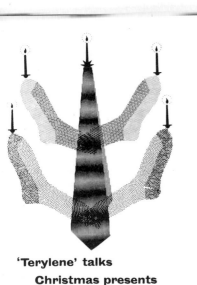

'Terylene' talks

Christmas presents

Ties and socks make ordinary presents, you think? Not if they're 100% 'Terylene'. Take 'Terylene' socks. They're soft. They're warm. They keep their shape — of course. But they are also unshrinkable. And they make sock darning seem very old fashioned.

A tie made entirely from 'Terylene' is also everything it should be — with important extras. It looks and feels very expensive indeed — a tie for an occasion only. In fact, it will cost far less than you'd expect to pay for such

qualities, and you can wear it day in, day out. It will come up smiling through all the trials that find an ordinary tie wanting. You can even wash it.

Nothing ordinary about 'Terylene' socks and ties. No present that sports a 'Terylene' label is an ordinary present.

'TERYLENE'

IMPERIAL CHEMICAL INDUSTRIES LIMITED · LONDON · S.W.4

Figure 4.4

LOOKING AT LABELS

|||| YOU WILL NEED: |||||||||||||||||||||||||||||||||||||||||||||||||||||||||||||||||||||||||||||||||||||||||||||||||||||
Selection of clothing and textile items
Pen and paper

1 Look at the labels on the items you have been given.

2 Write down the generic names of the fibres in the item.

3 Write down the percentage of each fibre present.

4 Write down any brand names.

Q 8
Which is the most common fibre in the class?

From now on only generic names will be used in this book. This is because they indicate clearly what a fibre is.

The problem of brand names does not often occur with natural fibres. These fibres have been well known for too many years and produced by too many people for a brand name to be established. However, organizations do exist to promote the use of these fibres. When they advertise they use the generic name.

Q 9
Name two organizations which promote the use of natural fibres.

4.3
WHAT IS TOP OF THE LEAGUE?
World fibre production in 1980 was about 30 million tonnes.

Q 10
Which fibre do you think is the most widely used?

Q 11
Estimate what percentage you think it is of total fibre production.

You probably guessed the fibre correctly but not the percentage production. This is because cotton is used for clothing in the highly populated developing countries and areas of the World like India and the Far East.

Figure 4.6 shows fibre usage for the World, for Western Europe, and for the United States. You can see some big differences.

Q 12
Look at the pie charts in figure 4.6 for the three areas. What can you say about:
a the use of cotton?
b the use of man-made fibres?
c the use of wool?

Although you could spend a lot of time analysing the statistics for the use of fibres, one thing is very clear: synthetic fibres are

Figure 4.5a and b
Everyday wear in India and China.

Figure 4.7
First advertisement for nylon, 1938.

Du Pont
for the World

a new word

NY

NO BETTER EXAMPLE of the fruits of research could be found than nylon—so new a material that a name had to be coined by Du Pont for it—so vast in the number of its possible uses that no list, however farseeing at present, can include them all—so promising in its first uses that Du Pont will spend $8,000,000 on a plant employing approximately 1,000 people.

Nylon is the generic name for all materials defined scientifically as synthetic fiber-forming polymeric amides having a

Figure 4.6
Pie charts of fibre usage in the World, Western Europe, and U.S.A. (1980).

very important, particularly in the United States and Western Europe. This is all the more surprising when you realize that the first synthetic fibre, nylon, was not produced commercially until 1938.

The graph in figure 4.8 shows that, although the amount of fibre used in the World has steadily increased, the percentage of synthetic fibre used each year has increased much more rapidly. Also, you can see from figure 4.6 that synthetics are more widely used in the developed countries of the World. It does seem that the richer the country, the more synthetic fibre it uses.

Q 13
Suggest some reasons why this might be so.

You might think that, if current trends continue, by the year 2000 the World will be near to using only synthetic fibres. However, it is always difficult to predict the future. You should remember that synthetic fibres are largely made from oil. What happens if the oil runs out?

The fibre which is top of the league in the West is cotton, with polyester very close behind. Wool, viscose, nylon, and acrylic are in the second division. The remaining fibres are in a minor league.

4.4
ANOTHER BIG DIFFERENCE BETWEEN FIBRES: PRICE
As you know, price is one of the three factors which decide choice. The price of the raw material (the fibre) affects the price of the finished product. Comparing the prices of fibres will help you to understand why some fibres are used more than others.

Figure 4.8
Graph showing the increase in use of synthetic fibres since 1938.

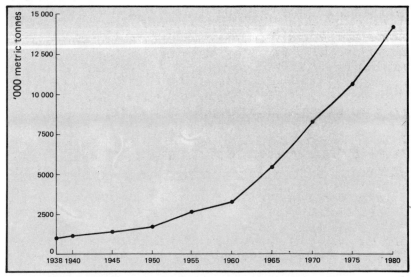

Q 14
What do you think affects the cost of producing a fibre?

Fibre manufacturers try to sell what they make for a profit. That is, the price they charge is more than their costs. How much profit they make depends on something economists call supply and demand. This is where aesthetics and performance come in.

The cost of producing a fibre can be affected by many other factors. For example, the weather can affect the price of natural fibres. So, working out the price of a fibre can be difficult. A fashion demand can make a particular aesthetic property so desirable that people will pay a lot of money for a particular garment, when a year or two previously no-one would have bought it. Denim jeans are an example of this.

Q 15
What would happen to the price of fibres in the following examples?
a Bad weather damages the *cotton* crop in a season when cotton is in big demand for denims and cords.
b A drought in Australia reduces the *wool* on the sheep, but people want winter clothing.
c The Arab oil-producing countries put up the price of *oil* but, because of the economic climate, people are buying fewer clothes.

Even though prices vary, some fibres are always more expensive than others as they cost more to produce. Table 4.2 is a guide to the relative cost of some common fibres.

Fibre	Price range
cotton	medium
wool	high
silk	very high
viscose	low
acetate	very low
triacetate	medium
nylon	medium
polyester	medium
acrylic	medium

Table 4.2

Figure 4.9
Denim.

BACKGROUND READING

THE SECRET OF THE WORM

Silk is the only usable fibre to be produced by an insect. This is the silk moth. It is usually called the silkworm because it is a worm-like larva — the young caterpillar stage of the insect's life cycle — which spins the silk. It wraps itself in a cocoon of silk and inside this changes into an adult moth. Then it bursts free of the cocoon and flies away. Several kinds of insect make silk cocoons, but the best silk comes from the true silk moth (its scientific name is *Bombyx mori*) which lives wild in China and feeds only on the leaves of the native Chinese white mulberry tree.

In China before 1000 B.C. people gathered the empty, burst cocoons and boiled them so that the strands of silk unravelled. Then they spun the short, broken fibres into thread and wove it into cloth. This is called 'wild silk' and is still made in several Eastern countries. Wild silk is rough and fairly cheap. Some kinds come from other insects. Even spider webs have sometimes been used.

In the ninth century B.C. some unknown Chinese found that if the cocoon was boiled before the insect escaped, the silk could be unravelled in a continuous strand up to 2.5 km long. This gave a very fine, strong, shiny fabric for which there was soon a great demand. People began to cultivate silkworms, feeding the larvae with mulberry leaves. The trade was strictly controlled by the Emperor. The process was kept secret.

Around the fifth century B.C. tribes of Asian horsemen, the Mongols, kept raiding China. The Chinese authorities bought them off, bribing them with the beautiful and expensive fabric. In this way silk became known outside China, and slowly an export trade began. Silk was carried to the West along the 'Silk Road', a trail which led through Central Asia and Persia (now Iran). The Romans knew of silk and paid enormous prices for it.

Naturally people in other countries wanted to make their own silk, but the secret of the worm was well kept. Anyway, few people would believe that an insect was the maker. There are many legends of how the secret was broken. Some say that a Chinese girl married a king of Khotan and smuggled silkworm eggs out of China hidden in her hair. Khotan (now Hotien) is near Kashmir, and certainly silk was being cultivated in the Indian region at an early time. Another story is that a Christian missionary returning from the East to Constantinople (now Istanbul) in A.D. 552 brought eggs in a bamboo medicine tube.

The insect was useless without the Chinese mulberry tree, for the larva would not thrive on any other food. When people realized this they had seeds brought and grew the trees. However, it was not until the seventeenth century that European silk cultivation got properly under way in France. Today most silk still comes from China, Japan, Thailand, and India.

Figure 4.10
Unwinding silk cocoons in seventeenth-century France.

29

CHAPTER 5
Producing the natural fibres

5.1
FROM PLANTATIONS AND GREEN FIELDS

The most widely used fibre in the World is cotton. It is not grown everywhere, but where it is grown it is an important part of the economy and culture of the area. Figure 5.1 (below) shows the most important cotton growing areas.

Cotton comes from a plant which is only able to grow in areas with certain weather conditions.

Q 1
Look at the map shown in figure 5.1. What do you think are the weather conditions which are needed to grow cotton successfully?

Cotton fibre is the hair attached to the seed in the seed *boll*. Figure 5.2 shows the cycle of cotton growth.

After the bolls are harvested the seeds are removed. The raw cotton is then baled and sent for sale. Figure 5.3 shows the processes.

As you know, wool is the hair from sheep. Figure 5.4 at the bottom of the next page shows the main areas where sheep are reared for their wool.

Figure 5.2a
Young cotton plants.

Figure 5.2b
Cotton flower.

Figure 5.2c
Cotton seed bolls.

Figure 5.1
Cotton growing areas of the World.

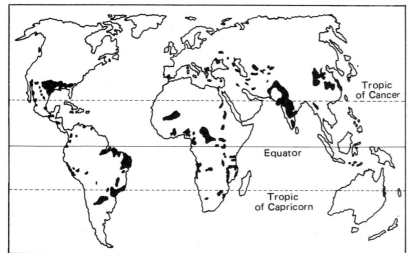

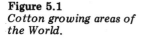

Figure 5.3a
Mechanical cotton picker.

Figure 5.3b
Cotton ginning machines which separate the cotton fibres from the seeds.

Figure 5.3c
Cotton in bales ready for shipping.

Figure 5.5
Woolsack (in front of the throne).

In the Middle Ages, England was one of the most important countries in the World for wool production. During this period there was not a single sheep in Australia. The wealth of England was built on wool and the Lord Chancellor sits on the 'woolsack' (figure 5.5) as a symbol of this.

The cycle of growth and production for Australian wool is shown in figure 5.6 on the next page.

Both cotton and wool are natural fibres. Weather conditions are not always favourable. Storms and drought, shortages of food, and many other factors may affect the growing cotton plant or the sheep. Because of this, different types of cotton plant and sheep are used in various parts of the World. This means there are variations in the quality of the fibre produced. By examining raw wool and raw cotton some of these variations can be seen.

EXAMINATION OF RAW WOOL AND COTTON FIBRES

||| YOU WILL NEED: ||||||||||||||||||||||||||||||||||||||||||||||||||||||||||||||||||||||||||||||||

Raw cotton fibres   Hand lens
Raw wool fibres   Dissecting needle
                          Ruler

1 Look at the samples of raw wool, first with the naked eye and then using the hand lens.

2 Look at the samples of raw cotton in the same way.

3 Remove individual fibres from both samples and examine them too.

Q 2
Are there any differences in shape and appearance between the wool and the cotton fibres?

Figure 5.4
Wool producing areas of the World.

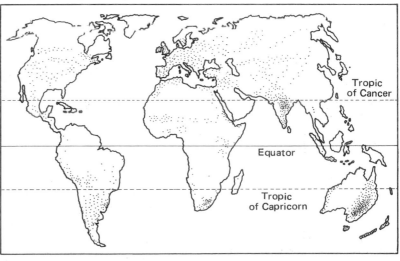

4 Take 10 fibres of wool and 10 fibres of cotton. Measure their lengths.

Q 3
Is there any difference between the lengths of the longest wool and the longest cotton fibres?

Q 4
Is there any difference in length between the individual cotton fibres?

Q 5
Is there any difference in length between the individual wool fibres?

Both the wool and the cotton fibres are relatively short in length. It is unlikely that any fibre will be more than 20 cm long. Some of the cotton fibres may be as short as 1 cm.

Relatively short fibres, like wool and cotton, are called *staple fibres*. However, wool fibres are generally longer than cotton fibres. Therefore wool is often called a *long staple fibre* and cotton a *short staple fibre*. There will also be a lot of difference in the lengths of the individual wool fibres and the lengths of the individual cotton fibres. You will probably have noticed that the cotton fibres are fairly straight and that the wool fibres are not. This is a special feature of a wool fibre. The term used to describe it is *crimp*.

The fibres you examined all came from one particular batch of wool or cotton, grown in a particular area. Differences occur in cotton and wool according to where they come from. Cotton fibres from the United States have an average length of about 2.5 cm; those from India are usually shorter. Egyptian and Sea Island cottons (from the West Indies) are generally longer. The longer fibres are usually finer and are made into fabrics with high aesthetic appeal. Wool quality is usually measured by the fineness of the fibres. The finest wool comes from the Merino sheep which is mainly reared in Australia. Coarser wools come from cross-bred sheep, such as those generally found in the United Kingdom. The finer wools are used for suitings and finer knitwear, whilst the coarsest wools are used for such things as carpets.

Figure 5.6a
Lambs.

Figure 5.6b
Sheep ready for shearing.

Figure 5.6c
Sheep shearing.

Figure 5.6e
Raw wool sales.

Figure 5.6d
Baling wool.

Figure 5.7
Cross-bred sheep.

5.2
THE USEFUL MOTH

The cultivation of silk was probably started by the Chinese nearly 3000 years ago (see the Background reading on page 29). The practice has spread, particularly in the Far East. Figure 5.8 shows the main areas of silk production or *sericulture*.

The production of silk depends on a moth, particularly a species known as *Bombyx mori* which lives on mulberry leaves. The cycle of production is shown in figure 5.9 on the next page.

EXAMINATION OF SILK FIBRES

||| YOU WILL NEED: |||||||||||||||||||||||||||||||||||||||||||||||||||||||||||||||||||||||||||||||||||||||||
Silk fibre sample   Hand lens or microscope

Using the hand lens or microscope examine the silk fibres.

Q 6
What is the most obvious difference between the silk fibres and the wool and cotton fibres you examined in section 5.1?

You will remember that wool and cotton are known as staple fibres. Because silk is long and continuous, it is known as a filament fibre or more usually as filament yarn.

Just like spiders, the silkworm larvae spin a continuous thread. Actually, although silk is a continuous thread, it is not one solid filament. The silkworm spins a strand from each of its two spinnerets, but these generally stick together and appear as a single (mono) filament. The producer winds threads from a number of cocoons together to give a multi-filament yarn.

The length of the yarn produced by the silkworm is often as much as 1000 metres, and can be as long as 2500 metres. Even though silk production can be controlled, its quality can vary because it is a natural fibre. Silk production is a skilled operation requiring many workers, so its production tends to be restricted to countries where labour costs are low. But it is still an expensive fibre.

Figure 5.8
Silk producing areas of the World.

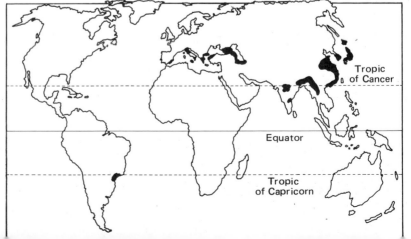

Q 7
Why do you think so little silk is produced in the United Kingdom?

5.3
THE BUILDING BLOCKS OF FIBRES
You have seen how three natural fibres are produced, but how are they built up? How does the cotton plant actually produce cotton fibre?

Plants grow by taking in food or nutrients from the soil and from the air with the help of the energy available from sunlight. The nutrients are changed by a series of chemical reactions to the actual chemicals which make up the plant itself. The process is called *photosynthesis*. In the case of the cotton plant, this will result in the production of the cotton boll. Therefore, the growth of the cotton boll is the result of the plant manufacturing new chemicals from the foodstuffs it takes in. Each part of the plant will be made up of a mixture of chemicals which will be unique to that part of the plant. Cotton fibre is therefore a mixture of chemicals. Most of it is a compound known as *cellulose*.

Cellulose is a polymer built up of thousands of units of the molecule glucose. As many as 10 000 molecules of glucose may join together in a chain to form a single molecule of cellulose in cotton. The cellulose molecule is a long chain. You can see how that shape resembles the shape of the fibre. Even though cellulose with its several thousand glucose units is a giant molecule, a molecule of cellulose is still incredibly small. It is not visible even to the most powerful optical microscope. Millions of cellulose molecules will be present in a single cotton fibre. The cellulose molecules are arranged in bundles or *fibrils*, and then the fibrils are arranged in groups to build up the fibre.

Figure 5.10
Cellulose molecules in a fibre.

Wool and silk are also polymers, but they are different from cotton. They are compounds called *proteins*. Once again the fibres are made up from polymer molecules. The shape of the molecule, that is, long and thin, is the same as that of the fibre itself. These are natural fibres. Suppose an attempt were made to manufacture a fibre artificially?

Q 8
What sort of chemical compound would be likely to produce a man-made fibre?

If the right chemical compound can be found, one other problem must be solved. Plants and animals have already solved it. A way must be found of growing or producing these molecules in a fibre form.

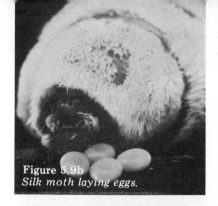
Figure 5.9b
Silk moth laying eggs.

Figure 5.9a
Adult silkmoth.

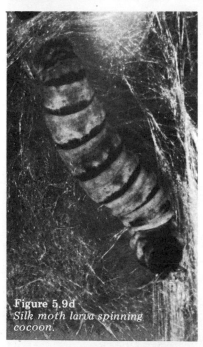
Figure 5.9d
Silk moth larva spinning cocoon.

Figure 5.9?
Silkworm on mulberry leaf.

Figure 5.11
From sheep to shoulder in record time.

BACKGROUND READING

FROM SHEEP TO SHOP

It is a long way from the natural wool coat of a sheep to a wool coat fit for you to wear. Sometimes, for a stunt, a garment has been completed from start to finish in a single day. To achieve this, each stage has to be carried out by a different expert. The World record of just over 4½ hours is for a sweater made in Scotland in 1976 — but this is unfair, because a knitted sweater can be made much more quickly than a proper woven, sewn garment. The record for a real woven coat stood at 13 hours in 1982. This is a remarkably short time when you consider the number of stages involved in making such a garment.

First the sheep is shorn. A skilled worker with electric clippers can sweep the whole fleece off in seconds. The raw wool is greasy and full of dirt and foreign bodies, so it must be washed. Next, it might be bleached and dyed. In fact dyeing can be done at any later stage if only a single colour is required. Sometimes wool or other natural fibres are left undyed in their original colour.

Once it is dry the wool is carded: that is, it is passed through a machine with combs which pull the tangled fibres out straight so that they can be spun into yarn. Often wool of different types or colours is spun together. To make a close woven coat fabric a yarn which is tight, hard, and strong is spun.

Now the yarn goes to the loom to be woven into cloth. For a coat a simple plain or twill weave would be used, perhaps with different coloured yarns to make designs such as checks or tartan. Most cloth is given a finishing treatment to produce a particular texture. It might be 'calendered' or 'milled' with rollers to felt the wool fibres together and make the surface smooth and dense. In the 'raising' process a stiff wire brush is used to pull up some fibres and make the fabric fuzzy. The cloth must also be stretched straight and flat, and then cleaned.

Now the cloth is cut out to make the pieces of the coat, using a pattern to give the shapes. The pattern pieces are arranged on the cloth so that the grain of the fabric runs the right way and there are no large, wasteful gaps. A woollen coat includes other cloths as well as the main wool one: a silk or viscose lining, a stiff interlining to shape the collar and lapels, and perhaps some padding in the shoulders, as well as trimmings, pocket linings, buttons, and so on. In mass produced clothes many thicknesses of cloth are cut out at once with a bandsaw or laser.

The pieces are then sewn together. In a cheap coat the job might be speeded up by using adhesives for some joins, or even heat welding for synthetic fabrics. Buttonholes are cut and bound. Trimmings and buttons are sewn on. The completed garment is pressed; then it is ready to wear.

CHAPTER 6
Man imitates nature

6.1
FIRST STAGE: PRODUCE THE SHAPE

The cotton plant and the sheep build up fibres step by step in the normal growth process. The silkworm produces a polymer in its body, in a liquid form, and then pumps it by muscle action through its spinnerets to produce the silk yarn.

This suggests that if a man-made fibre is to be produced there is a choice of two methods which could be used to give the correct shape — once a suitable polymer has been found.

Q 1
Which of these two methods would be easier for a manufacturer to copy?

6.2
REGENERATING THE NATURAL POLYMER

There are two problems involved in producing a man-made fibre. The first is finding a polymer and the second is producing the correct shape. Cellulose is the main chemical in cotton and is an important part of all plants. Man-made fibres could be made from a naturally occurring polymer if a way could be found of reprocessing it into the correct shape.

Q 2
What would need to be done to the cellulose from plants so that it could be used to produce a man-made fibre? (Remember that the means of getting the shape is by imitating the way in which a silkworm produces silk, that is, pumping the polymer material through its spinnerets.)

Figure 6.1

Count Hilaire Chardonnet.

The first person to think of a way to do this was Count Hilaire Chardonnet.

The process generally used today is the viscose process discovered in 1891 by the British scientists Cross and Bevan. In this process, cellulose from wood pulp is dissolved using chemicals (caustic soda and carbon disulphide) to produce a thick solution. A thick liquid is often called a *viscous* liquid. This is the origin of the name of the fibre produced: viscose rayon, or viscose. The solution is forced through a spinneret (that is, it is *extruded*) into a vessel containing sulphuric acid. The sulphuric acid removes the chemicals used to dissolve the cellulose and the cellulose is *regenerated* (that is, made again) in the correct fibre shape. This process of regenerating is called *wet spinning*, because the fibre is produced by *extruding* it into a liquid (the sulphuric acid).

Although viscose is made from cellulose, the method of producing the fibre shape from the polymer solution is clearly not the same as the way the shape is made by the cotton plant. Viscose is *similar* to cotton in many ways, but it is not *identical*. One big difference is that the number of molecules of glucose in the average chain of a cellulose molecule is much less in viscose than in cotton.

What property of the fibre will this difference affect?

6.3
CHANGING IT A BIT
Viscose is a successful man-made fibre which is produced using a natural polymer, cellulose, and copying the shape-producing method of the silkworm. The next stage is to modify the polymer to give different fibres.

The starting point is cellulose because cellulose is readily available and cheap. Today this has a particular advantage in a World concerned with the usage of limited resources, like oil, which cannot be renewed. Cellulose from plants is a renewable resource. Even before Chardonnet first produced spun viscose from dissolved cellulose it was known that cellulose could be treated with acetic acid to give different chemical compounds. Later it was shown that these compounds could be spun, like viscose, into fibres.

Depending on the amount of acetic acid added to the cellulose, either secondary acetate, usually called just acetate, or triacetate fibre can be produced.

There is an important difference between the spinning of acetate and triacetate and the spinning of viscose. The chemical, known as the solvent, which is used to dissolve the polymer from which acetate and triacetate are made, evaporates easily in warm air. Therefore when the fibres are spun by pumping the dissolved polymer through the spinneret, instead of pumping them into a

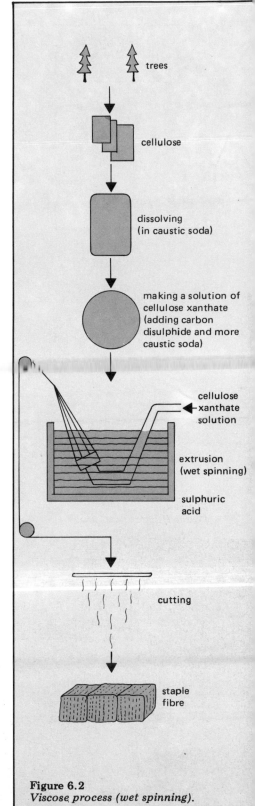

Figure 6.2
Viscose process (wet spinning).

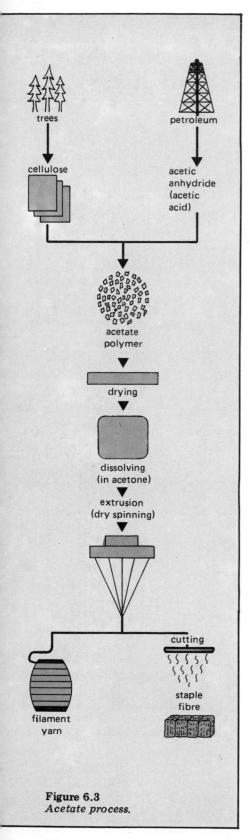

Figure 6.3
Acetate process.

liquid they are simply pumped into the air. The solvent is allowed to evaporate thus leaving the solid fibre. This process is called *dry spinning*. Figure 6.3 shows this process.

6.4
SYNTHETIC POLYMERS

So far, the man-made fibres you have considered are regenerated from a natural polymer. A polymer could also be produced artifically. This is what is done with polyester, nylon, and acrylic. Even here, the original source is naturally occurring. It is oil. The polymer is made by using simple chemical compounds which come from oil and joining them together or *synthesizing* the polymer, hence the term *synthetic fibre*. Polyester is usually made by synthesizing the polymer from ethylene glycol and terephthalic acid. If you think of ethylene glycol as Compound A and terephthalic acid as Compound B, in the process one molecule of A joins to one molecule of B and then a large number of the molecules formed, AB, join in a chain to give a polymer as shown below.

Molecule A + Molecule B

These join to give A—B—A—B—A—B—A—B—A—B—A—B
Figure 6.4

The discovery of polyester was made by two British chemists, Whinfield and Dickson in 1941.

Nylon is produced in two main ways. The first method, discovered by Carothers in the United States in 1935, gave the first truly synthetic fibre. Hexamethylenediamine and adipyl chloride react together to form the nylon polymer. Like polyester, if hexamethylenediamine is thought of as Compound C and adipyl chloride as Compound D, one molecule each of C and D combine first and then continue combining to give a long chain polymer, that is the nylon (or polyamide) polymer.

Q 4
Draw a diagram to show the structure of a nylon polymer
using the letters C and D to represent the chemicals involved.

A second form of nylon is made from a single chemical, caprolactam. Here the compound can be made to link up with itself so giving a polymer. Although the two forms of nylon (the first called nylon 6.6 and the second nylon 6) are slightly different chemically, their properties in clothing are virtually identical.

Acrylic polymer is mainly produced by polymerizing a chemical compound, again derived from oil, acrylonitrile.

You now have three synthetic polymers (assuming that the two nylons are the same) which are available for forming fibres. Because they differ chemically, their properties will be different from each other and also they will differ from the natural fibres, and from the regenerated fibres.

These polymers must now be made into fibre shapes. The nylon and polyester polymers are obtained as solid plastic materials. These can be melted so they do not need to be dissolved in any other chemicals. The melted polymers can be pumped through a spinneret to give the fibres which solidify in the air. This is called *melt spinning*. Figure 6.5 shows the process of polyester production.

Acrylic polymer cannot be converted into fibre by melt spinning. It can be dissolved in chemicals and wet spun, like viscose, or dry spun, like acetate or triacetate.

6.5
GETTING IT STRAIGHT
The fibres when spun from the polymer are made up of millions of molecules. These molecules themselves are long chains and so are similar to the fibre in shape. If the molecules are lined up in the fibre in the same direction, there will be a greater amount of contact between the molecules, so giving a stronger fibre. It will also be more even. Unfortunately, when you first make the fibres they have a random (haphazard) arrangement of molecules, that is they have *low orientation* (see figure 6.6).

The molecules in the fibre have to be arranged so that they are nearly parallel to each other, that is, they become *highly orientated*. This is shown in figure 6.7.

Figure 6.6

Figure 6.7

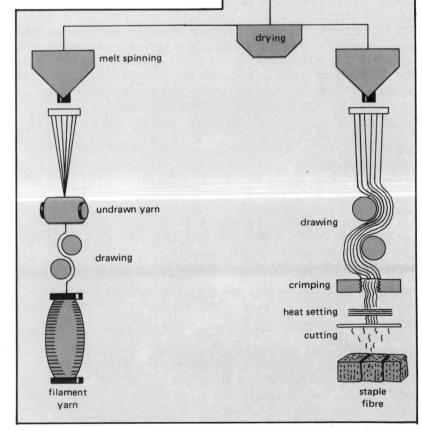

Figure 6.5
Polyester process.

You can achieve this high orientation after spinning by stretching the fibres in a process called *drawing*. By controlling the amount of drawing, the required amount of orientation can be obtained so giving the best fibre properties.

Try drawing a fibre yourself.

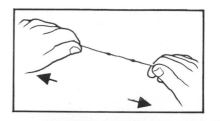

DRAWING THE UNDRAWN FIBRE

IIII YOU WILL NEED: IIIIIIIIIIIIIIIIIIIIIIIIIIIIIIIIIIIIIIIIIIIIIIIIIIIIIIIIIIIIIIIIIIIIIIIIIIIIII
Sample of undrawn fibre
Ruler

1 Measure the sample of undrawn fibre.

2 Now stretch (draw) the sample, as shown in figure 6.8 above.

Q 5
What happens to the fibre along its length?

Q 6
What happens to the width of the fibre?

Q 7
What is the final length of the fibre?

Q 8
Calculate the percentage increase in the length of the fibre.

The control on fibre properties illustrated by the drawing process shows an important difference between man-made and natural fibres. Big variations can occur in natural fibres because the growing process is difficult to control. Man-made fibre production can be carefully controlled so that there need be no variation in the quality of the fibre produced.

6.6
ONE MORE STAGE

Man-made fibres are made by imitating the action of the silk-worm, so the fibre is produced in filament form. There is no limit to the possible length of yarn a factory could produce, but in practice only a limited amount can be wound onto a package such as the bobbins in figure 6.9. The yarn could contain any number of individual filaments.

Q 9
How could the number of filaments present in a particular yarn be increased or decreased?

Man-made fibre manufacturers produce yarns in a range of different thicknesses for different purposes. The fibre may also be required in short lengths to be like the staple fibres of cotton or wool. To do this is easy for the man-made fibre producer. The filament yarn is simply cut up to the length which is needed. Man-made fibres are therefore available in both staple and filament form. Table 6.1 shows examples of their uses.

Figure 6.8 (left)
Drawing the undrawn fibre.

Figure 6.9
Bobbins of filament yarn on knitting machines.

Fibre	Form	Examples of use
Polyester	staple	blended with cotton for sheets
	filament	jersey fabric
Viscose	staple	blended with polyester for trousers
	filament	linings (little used)
Acetate	staple	not used
	filament	blouse fabrics
Triacetate	staple	not used
	filament	dress and blouse fabrics
Nylon	staple	carpets
	filament	tights
Acrylic	staple	knitwear
	filament	not used

Table 6.1

For clothing, polyester is used in both forms; nylon mainly in filament form; acetate and triacetate entirely in filament form; and viscose mainly, and acrylic entirely, in staple form.

6.7
DISTINGUISHING BETWEEN THEM

Although all fibres are made up of polymers, the polymers do differ from one another — except in the case of cotton and viscose. Here it is the fibre-forming processes, one natural and one artificial, which produce differences in the cellulose molecules. Sometimes it is necessary to be able to distinguish between fibres. There are some obvious differences: for instance some are filament and some are staple.

Q 10
Can you tell the difference between fibres just by looking at them or handling them?

It is fairly easy to distinguish between some fibres, but it is more difficult if the fibres have been spun into yarn and the yarn made into fabric. Simple looking and handling methods give a judgment based mainly on aesthetics, which is not reliable. In a fabric, the finish or any colour can easily disguise the fibre appearance. Chemical tests or more accurate physical tests are needed.

A simple test which can be done to distinguish between many fibres is to burn them.

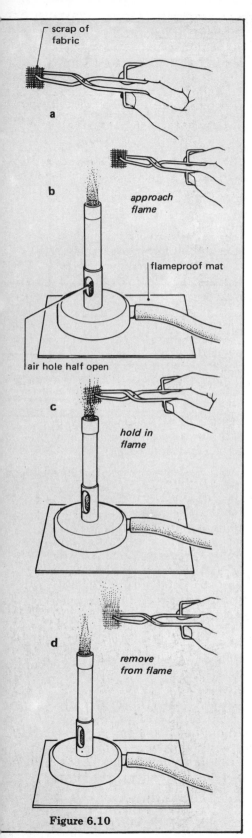

a

b approach flame

flameproof mat

air hole half open

c hold in flame

d remove from flame

Figure 6.10

scrap of fabric

DISTINGUISHING FIBRES BY BURNING TESTS

||| YOU WILL NEED: ||||||||||||||||||||||||||||||||||||||||||||||||||||||||||||||

Samples of pure fibres or small scraps of fabrics

Pair of crucible tongs or tweezers
Bunsen burner
Flameproof mat or tray of sand

1 Take a small sample of the given fibre and hold it firmly in the crucible tongs or tweezers.

2 Light the Bunsen burner with a taper. Adjust the flame by opening the air hole about one half, so that the flame is blue but not roaring.

3 Observe the behaviour of the fibres as they
   a approach the flame
   b are held in the flame
   c are removed from the flame.

Here are some observations you might make.

1 The fibre melts.
2 The fibre shrivels away from the flame.
3 The fibre itself burns. If it does, the flame could be smoky or clear.
4 When the fibre is removed from the flame it might go out or carry on burning.
5 The fibre develops a hard bead when it is removed from the flame.
6 The fibre has a crumbly ash when it is removed from the flame.
7 There is a smell given off when the fibre is burned.
8 You may recognize the smell as being similar to one you have smelled before — for example, burnt paper or burnt hair.

Write down what you see in a table like figure 6.11.

This is a chemical test because burning is a chemical reaction between a substance, in this case the fibre, and the oxygen in the air. Many fibres may be identified in this way.

Q 11
Which fibres would you find it difficult to distinguish between with the burning test?

You could have difficulty deciding which fibre was present if it was dyed or if there was more than one fibre. A more exact method is to use a microscope. To the eye many fibres look identical, but examined under the microscope each fibre has its own special features.

EXAMINATION OF FIBRES UNDER A MICROSCOPE

||| YOU WILL NEED: ||||||||||||||||||||||||||||||||||||||||||||||||||||||||||||||

Samples of fibres
Glycerol in dropper bottle

Microscope
Coverslips
Microscope slides

Fibre	Reaction of fibre:		
	when approaching the flame	when held in the flame	when removed from the flame
polyester	melts and shrivels away from flame	burns with smoky flame	usually stops burning, leaving a hard, dark-coloured bead

1 Make up a slide using a small quantity of a given fibre.

Figure 6.11

2 Put the slide under the microscope and examine it under the low power lens.

3 When you have found a good section of the fibre to look at, turn to a higher magnification. Finally look at the fibre under the highest possible magnification on your microscope.

Look at your fibre sample under high magnification and draw what you can see. Now compare what you have drawn with the examples shown in figure 6.12 on the next page. These are a guide to the characteristics of each fibre. Can you identify these characteristics on your fibre sample?

BACKGROUND READING

'MADE FROM COAL, AIR, AND WATER'

Nylon was not one of those accidental discoveries. It was found mainly through hard work backed by plenty of money — though of course luck also played a part. In 1927 the giant American Du Pont chemical corporation set aside $250 000 (then worth far more) for research into new substances and invited Dr Wallace Carothers, a scientist from Harvard University, to lead the programme.

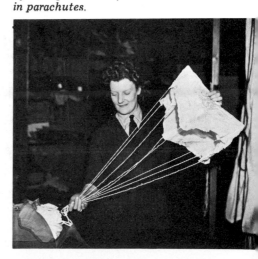

Figure 6.13
During the Second World War nylon replaced silk for use in parachutes.

Carothers chose to work on polyesters, a group of plastics which then had no practical use. In 1930 a fellow worker, Dr Julian Hill, noticed that one kind could be drawn into a long strand. But although Carothers tried hard to make a useful fibre from it, he could not. He gave up, but a few months later he was persuaded to start again.

He turned to a different group of substances, the polyamides, and this time he got results. It took until 1935 to develop a workable process for making polyamide fibre. By 1937 Du Pont had started large-scale production. They called the fibre Nylon, which was meant to suggest that it was a 'new rayon'.

In 1939 nylon stockings were launched at the New York World's Fair. The advertising slogan used was 'Made from coal, air, and water'. Four million pairs were sold in the first four days, and

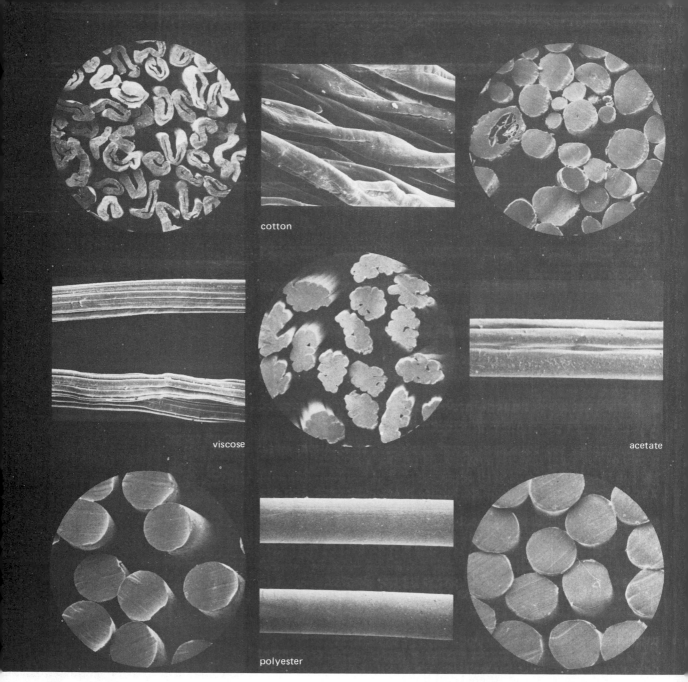

cotton

viscose

acetate

polyester

Figure 6.12
Longitudinal view and cross-section of fibres under magnification. Note the scales on wool, the 'twisted ribbon' of cotton, the regular longitudinal shapes of the man-made fibres, and the regular cross-sections of the synthetics.

during the whole year 64 million. The new stockings were tougher than the former silk ones, and also cheaper. (Incidentally, most modern nylon is made from oil, not coal.)

During the Second World War supplies of silk from the Far East were cut off. This was serious, not so much for stockings but for airmen's parachutes, which until then had been made from silk. Nylon, now made in Britain as well as in the United States, proved even better. It was also used for glider tow ropes, tyre cords for large aircraft, inflatable life rafts, and some solid mouldings. There was also a large British black market in American nylon stockings brought over by servicemen.

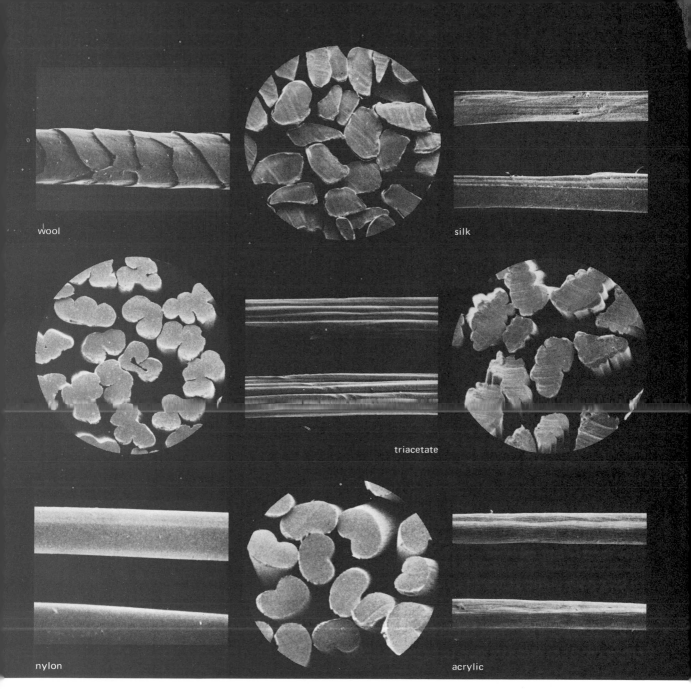

wool

silk

triacetate

nylon

acrylic

After the war nylon found more and more uses. An important
one was the first drip-dry shirts, which came in during the 1950s.
Nylon was and is used mainly for fibres and fabrics, but solid
nylon mouldings can outperform those made from other
materials. For example, curtains can be hung on nylon rails with
nylon hooks which glide smoothly, replacing old-fashioned
metal wheels and runners. Both in solid and in fibre form nylon
is extremely tough. Nylon mooring ropes, used on oil rigs in the
stormy North Sea, are the strongest of any kind. In the home,
nylon carpets outwear woollen ones. Another advantage which
nylon has is that it does not burn readily, and when it does burn,
it does not give off poisonous fumes.

CHAPTER 7
Comparing the fibres

7.1
WHAT TO COMPARE?

You know from Chapter 4 what the main fibres used for clothing are. The important differences in the properties of these fibres are those which show up when they are made into clothing and worn. In this chapter you will look at the properties which matter to the consumer and carry out investigations to test them. The properties are divided into aesthetic and performance properties.

Aesthetic properties are concerned with handle and appearance. Performance properties relate to what you expect when you wear a garment and when the garment is cleaned.

Q 1
Think back to the work you did in Chapter 1. What performance properties are important when considering a garment?

Many of your answers will be to do with how long a garment will last. This property is called *durability*. You might have mentioned the question of whether or not a garment will keep its shape, whether it will crease or wrinkle, and whether it will bag at the knees. This is called *shape retention*. Another important property is *size retention*. Will the garment shrink or stretch? Both shape and size retention have to be examined not only when the garment is worn but also when it is cleaned. (When you ask if a garment is washable you are not asking if you can put it in the washing machine and wash it. You are asking whether it will look the same and be the same size after washing.)

When you wash a garment it is important to know how quickly it will dry. Therefore the *water absorption* of the fabric is important. This property also affects how comfortable the garment is to wear, and how easily it becomes dirty.

Keeping warm or cool matters, so the *insulation* properties of the fibre must be considered.

Finally there is a property which you have already compared in section 6.7. This is the *flammability* of the fibres. (Remember that this means the same as *inflammability*.) You have already observed that there are differences between the fibres in this respect.

Figure 7.1
The important properties of fibres.

FLAMMABILITY

INSULATION

SIZE RETENTION

46

Figure 7.2

WATER ABSORPTION

DURABILITY

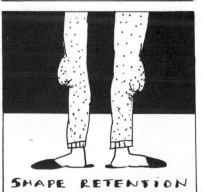

SHAPE RETENTION

7.2
HOW TO COMPARE

The consumer is interested in both aesthetic and performance properties, so the fibres have to be tested for these. However, people buy clothes or textile items not fibres. Therefore any tests should be carried out not on the fibres but on the clothes made from those fibres. In practice, as you saw in Chapter 2, the main part of the garment is the main body fabric. However, where an important trimming is present this may have to be tested as well if the total performance of the garment is to be assessed. (See Chapter 13.)

In comparing fibres by testing fabrics, you must remember that fibres are converted to fabrics by a number of processes. These processes enable a whole variety of fabrics to be produced from the same fibre. Figure 7.2 (above) shows some of the different things which are made from wool.

Q 2
Make a list of all the fabrics you can think of which are made from cotton fibre. An example to help you is cotton velvet.

If you are comparing different fibres you must compare fabrics made from them in a similar way and of a similar weight. For example, you know that a heavy wool fabric will last longer than a lightweight one. So if you were comparing wool and another fibre for durability you would use fabric of the same weight for both the fibres being tested.

In the comparisons you will make, it is important to realize that all the fibres being considered are used successfully in commercial practice. Even if some fibres appear inferior to others in certain properties, they may be perfectly satisfactory in the right fabric and the right garment.

7.3
AESTHETICS FIRST

The difficulty of comparing aesthetics is that you cannot measure factors such as handle and appearance. You tend to like it or dislike it.

COMPARING AESTHETIC FACTORS

The comparisons you make between the nine fabrics will be your own personal opinion.

‖‖ YOU WILL NEED: ‖‖‖
Fabric samples

1 Compare the handle of the fabrics, that is, how they feel. You might use words like smooth, slippery, or rough, to describe the feel.

2 Look at the appearance of the fabrics. Are they dull or shiny? Do they have a soft or hard look?

3 How do the fabrics drape, that is, how do they hang? Do they fall into soft folds or are they stiff?

Chapter 2 gives more detail about tests you can do to help you make up your mind.

4 Record your opinions on a table like figure 7.3.

5 Now compare this with the opinions of the rest of the class.

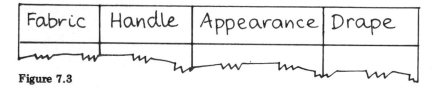

Fabric	Handle	Appearance	Drape

Figure 7.3

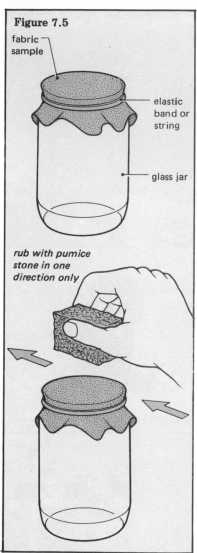

Figure 7.5

fabric sample

elastic band or string

glass jar

rub with pumice stone in one direction only

Figure 7.4

7.4
HOW LONG WILL IT LAST?

When you wear a garment you are obviously concerned about how long it will be before a hole or tear appears in it. Why does a fabric break down? It may be that the yarns in the fabric become separated. It could be that the fibres become separated from each other in the yarn. The fibres themselves may be damaged or split. Finally the molecules making up the fibre could be broken down. How can this happen? Firstly there are a whole variety of physical wearing effects on a garment. You can rub the fabric against a surface. This is termed *abrasion*.

Q 3
At what points on a garment is abrasion likely to occur fairly often? (Look at figure 7.4.)

COMPARING THE ABRASION RESISTANCE OF SAMPLE FABRICS

||| YOU WILL NEED: |||||||||||||||||||||||||||||||||||||||||||||||||||||||||||||||||||||||||||||||||||||||||||||||||||||||||||||||||||||||||||

9 sample fabrics

Cocoa tin or jam jar
Pumice stone
Rubber band or string

1 Put a sample of fabric over the neck of the tin or jar (as in figure 7.5).

2 Hold in place, very firmly, using the elastic band or string.

3 Rub the pumice stone over the stretched sample in one direction only using slow regular movement.

4 Count the number of rubs before the first sign of a hole appears.

5 Record your results in a table.

Now place the fabrics in order of resistance to abrasion. The least durable will be at number 1 and the most durable at number 9.

Other physical strains which affect a garment are tearing, pulling, and flexing. Figure 7.6 shows common examples of these three strains. (The amount of pulling a fabric will take is called its *tensile* strength.)

Because of the variety of strains, the comparison of durability is complicated. Different fibres and different fabric constructions can react in different ways. In the tests for physical factors in wear, the synthetic fibres polyester and nylon generally appear better than the natural fibres, but this is only part of the story. All fibres are chemicals and can be attacked by other chemicals, even those produced by the body such as perspiration.

All fibres are finally destroyed by excessive heat, and all fibres are broken down or degraded by the action of sunlight. Sunlight is one of the chief reasons why textile fabrics wear out.

Q 4

Think of a use of textiles where the fact that they are weakened or degraded by sunlight would be of particular importance.

You can see that forecasting durability is very difficult. You can list the problems you have to consider.

1 The fabrics are constantly being subjected to physical wear.

2 Initially, the fibres differ in strength.

3 The fabrics are constantly subjected to chemical degradation and often to sunlight.

4 The fibres differ in their resistance to chemical attack and sunlight.

Figure 7.6a
Tearing action.

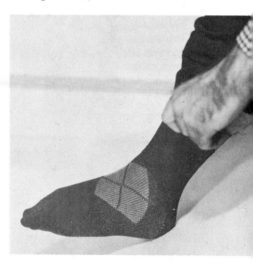

Figure 7.6b
Tensile action.

Figure 7.6c
Flexing action.

Synthetic fibres are generally more resistant to both physical and chemical degradation than natural fibres. A table of approximate order of durability can be made (figure 7.7).

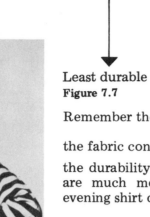

Most durable	nylon, polyester
	silk
	wool
	acrylic
	cotton
	viscose
Least durable	triacetate, acetate

Figure 7.7

Remember these two points:

the fabric construction can have a great effect;

the durability requirements of a garment such as a work overall are much more severe than those of a garment such as an evening shirt or blouse.

So a fabric which is unsuitable for tough conditions can be perfectly suitable for others, because performance is not the only factor which matters. Aesthetics and price matter as well.

(Flammability is a performance factor. Use worksheet FM4 to discover how different fibres react to burning.)

7.5
STAYING IN GOOD SHAPE

To stay in good shape, a garment or fabric must not shrink or stretch during wear or cleaning. A number of fibres can have shrinking problems but if the fabric is made and finished correctly these can be overcome. The exception is wool. Wool tends to shrink badly when you wash it. This is due to the structure of the wool fibre itself. When you looked at wool fibres under the microscope (Chapter 6) you saw that the fibre was covered in overlapping scales. When wool is washed, the action of the water and the agitation cause the fibres to move and slip over each other, but the interlocking of the scales causes a gradual decrease in size. This is called *felting*.

This is why when you wash wool you should do it very carefully. A new finishing treatment to overcome the problem will be discussed in Chapter 12.

Although a garment can keep its overall size it can lose its shape. One of the easiest ways for this to happen is that it becomes wrinkled or creased. Every fabric will wrinkle or crease under certain conditions, because of the soft, draping qualities of textiles. For example, if you bend your arm or knee you will produce creasing. What matters is how quickly the fabric recovers from creasing. If it does not recover quickly it will not look good. The best way to restore its appearance is to iron the garment.

Figure 7.8
The effect of felting on a sweater.

50

Compare the crease or wrinkle recovery of similar fabrics made from different fibres.

IIII YOU WILL NEED: IIIIIIIIIIIIIIIIIIIIIIIIIIIIIIIIIIIIIIIIIIIIIIIIIIIIIIIIIIIIIIIIIIIIIIIIIIIIIIIIIIIIIIIIIIIIIIIIIIIIIIIIIIII
9 sample fabrics
Clock or watch with seconds hand

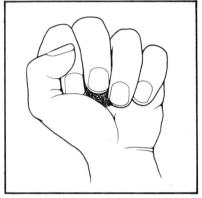

1 Crease or wrinkle the fabric as shown in figure 7.9.

2 Hold the fabric in your hand for 10 seconds.

3 Let the fabric go and observe how easily the fabric recovers.

4 Make observations after 1 minute, 2½ minutes, and 5 minutes. (Use a scale for assessment from 1 to 5 where 1 remains badly creased and wrinkled and 5 returns to almost perfect flat form.)

5 Put the fibres into order from best recovery to worst recovery.

Creasing does not always occur with dry fabrics. It can occur in wet conditions, such as when the fabric is being washed. Fibres can behave very differently under these conditions.

Compare the crease or wrinkle recovery of the fabric samples when wet.

Figure 7.9

IIII YOU WILL NEED IIIIIIIIIIIIIIIIIIIIIIIIIIIIIIIIIIIIIIIIIIIIIIIIIIIIIIIIIIIIIIIIIIIIIIIIIIIIIIIIIIIIIIIIIIIIIIIIIIIIIIIIIIIIIIIIIIIIIIIIIIIIIIIII
9 fabric samples (the same ones as before)
Water plus a *little* detergent in a bowl

Clock or watch with seconds hand
Iron and ironing-board

1 Iron the fabric samples.

2 Put some lukewarm water into a bowl and add a little detergent.

3 Soak the fabric samples in the water for 5 minutes.

4 Carry out the creasing tests in exactly the same way as you did before, but this time using the wet samples.

5 Observe the crease or wrinkle recovery after 1 minute, 2½ minutes, and 5 minutes and record the results using the same scale of values.

Q 5
a Which fabrics show the most difference in performance?
b Which fabrics show almost no change?

Fabrics which recover well from creasing when wet can be made into garments which need little or no ironing after washing. They would therefore be the minimum iron, minimum care, permanent press, or easy care fabrics.

Q 6
Do the results from your tests correspond with what you know of fabrics that need little or no ironing after washing? Discuss this with your teacher.

ANOTHER PART OF GOOD SHAPE
Some garments require a crease or pleat in them.

Q 7
Name two garments in which it would be an advantage to have a permanent crease or pleat.

The need for this crease or pleat is to give an acceptable appearance. Keeping in good shape for these garments means keeping a sharp crease or pleat under all wearing or cleaning conditions. All fibres can be set into a crease or pleat but most will lose the crease very quickly especially when washed.

Compare pleat retention in similar fabrics made from different fibres.

IIII YOU WILL NEED: IIIIIIIIIIIIIIIIIIIIIIIIIIIIIIIIIIIIIIIIIIIIIIIIIIIIIIIIIIIIIIIIIIIIIIIIIIIIIIIIII

9 samples of fabrics
9 sets of pleat formers
String (not polypropylene type)

Clock
Oven (preheated to 160 °C)
Spray bottle
Bowl of hand-hot soapy water
Knife

Make two pleat formers as shown in figure 7.10.

1 Mark the fabric samples A to I to identify them.

2 Lightly spray the fabrics with water and put the fabric between two pleat formers (see figure 7.11).

3 Fold the pleat formers and tie securely with string.

4 Put the pleat formers in the oven for 20 minutes, then remove and allow to cool.

5 Remove the fabrics from the pleat formers and cut the fabrics in half.

6 Wash one half of each of the fabrics in a soapy solution of hand hot water for a few minutes. Rinse in cold water.

7 Allow the fabrics to dry on a flat surface.

8 Compare and assess the pleat retention of the unwashed and washed samples of the fabrics. Use a scale of 1 to 5, where 1 = pleats virtually completely removed and 5 = pleats virtually identical to the unwashed sample.

9 Make a table of the order of pleat retention, the best being placed first, the worst last.

To sum up, the best shape retention performance is usually obtained from nylon and polyester. Wool is good under dry conditions but wrinkles badly when wet. Cotton and other fibres derived from cellulose have a generally lower performance.

7.6
WATER ABSORPTION
When a fabric gets wet, water is trapped between the yarns and between the fibres in the yarns. Water can also be absorbed by

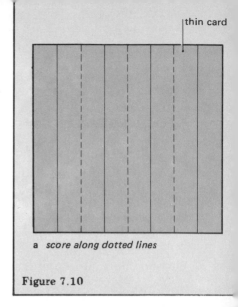

a   *score along dotted lines*

Figure 7.10

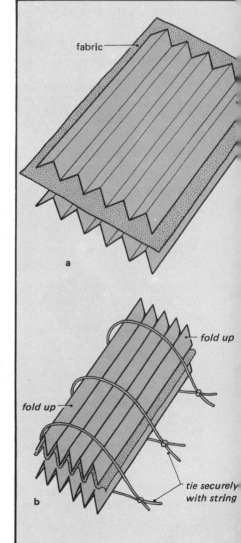

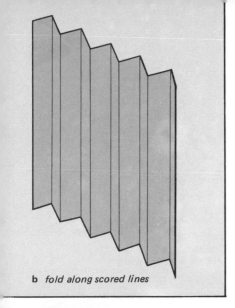

b *fold along scored lines*

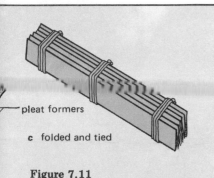

pleat formers

c folded and tied

Figure 7.11
Putting the fabric in the pleat former.

Figure 7.13

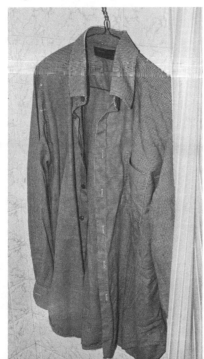

the fibres themselves and it is here that the fibres differ. All fabrics get wet but those where the fibres do not absorb water will dry more quickly.

Q 8
You will have heard of the term 'drip-dry'. What does this mean?

A fibre which absorbs water is called a *hydrophilic* fibre. One which does not absorb water is known as a *hydrophobic* fibre. In practice every fibre absorbs some moisture, but some absorb very much more than others. The order for absorption for the fibres is shown in figure 7.12.

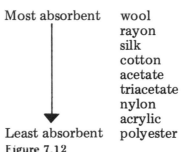

Most absorbent	wool
	rayon
	silk
	cotton
	acetate
	triacetate
	nylon
	acrylic
Least absorbent	polyester

Figure 7.12

The fabrics made from triacetate, acrylic, nylon, and polyester are generally regarded as drip-dry. It is this property which has enabled drip-dry clothing to be developed. You can test this in an experiment.

Measure the rate of drying of similar fabrics made from different fibres.

|||| YOU WILL NEED: |||||||||||||||||||||||||||||||||||||||||||||||||||||||||||||||||||||||||||||||||||
9 fabric samples
Bowl of water plus one 15-ml (table) spoon of detergent

Line and clothes pegs
Tumble drier
Balance for weighing

1 Put the fabric samples (previously marked A to I for identification) into the tumble drier for 5 minutes to ensure that they are thoroughly dry.

2 Remove from the drier, then cool and weigh each sample. Record the weight.

3 Wash the samples for 5 minutes in hand hot soapy water. Remove and rinse.

4 Peg on line and allow to drip for 15 minutes.

5 Weigh the samples again and record the weight.

You can now work out the percentage of water remaining in each sample, using the following formula.

$$\frac{\text{Weight of washed sample} - \text{weight of original sample}}{\text{Weight of original sample}} \times 100 =$$

% water remaining in sample

Make a table to show the order of retention of water.

Although quickness of drying is an obvious advantage, the ability to absorb moisture can also be an advantage. Your body constantly gives off water as perspiration, particularly during exercise. Fibres which absorb moisture therefore keep you more comfortable (figure 7.15).

You are probably all familiar with the problem of static charges which can build up on garments. The presence of water in the fibres allows the static electricity to leak away more easily. Static electricity attracts dust and so fabrics with low moisture absorbency tend to retain more static. Worksheet FM17 explains this and shows the effect of fabric softeners.

Compare the dust pick-up of similar fabrics made from different fibres.

Figure 7.14
Fabric attracting dust.

Figure 7.15

IIII **YOU WILL NEED:** IIIIIIIIIIIIIIIIIIIIIIIIIIIIIIIIIIIIIIIIIIIIIIIIIIIIIIIIIIIIIIIIIIIIIIIIIIIIIIIIII
9 fabric samples plus a sample of anti-static nylon
Loose dust from a cleaner

1 Take each fabric sample and rub it over your knee for 10 seconds.

2 Hold the sample over the dust about 3 cm away.

3 Observe the pick-up of dust with each sample. (The fabric in figure 7.14 has attracted dust.)

4 Divide the fabrics into the following categories: large pick-up, moderate pick-up, and small pick-up.

Q 9
Do the results from this test relate to what you found out about water retention?

Do your results fit in with what has been said about water absorbency being related to static electricity and hence the attraction of dust?

7.7
KEEPING WARM AND KEEPING COOL
Human beings generally need protection from outside temperature. In many climates, clothing has an important part to play which is not related to aesthetic factors.

If the clothes you are wearing are poor conductors of heat (that is, good insulators) they will keep you warm. But clothes are made of fibres. So you might think that all you need to find out is which fibre is the worst conductor (that is, the best insulator) and you would know what would be best to use to make a winter coat. But you would be wrong. As you will see in Chapter 8, the greatest part of a fabric consists of air trapped by the fibres. Depending on how the fabric has been made, as much as 80 per cent can be air.

Fortunately air itself is a poor conductor of heat so the way a textile fabric works to keep the body warm is to trap a layer of air, which then acts as an insulator. The conductive properties of the fibre therefore matter very little. What matters is how thick the fabric is. The thicker the fabric, the more air is trapped and the better the insulation.

Test the insulation properties of different fabrics.

IIII YOU WILL NEED: IIIIIIIIIIIIIIIIIIIIIIIIIIIIIIIIIIIIIIIIIIIIIIIIIIIIIIIIIIIIIIIIIIIIIIIIIIIIIIIIIIIIIIIIIIIIIIIIIIIIIII
9 fabric samples plus 2 heavyweight fabrics
Cotton wool

11 boiling-tubes
Test-tube rack
Clock or watch with seconds hand
Kettle for boiling water
Thermometer (-10 to $110\,^\circ$C)

1 Fit the fabric sample tightly around the boiling-tube so that half of the tube is covered.

2 Put the tube in the test-tube rack. Put a thermometer into it.

3 Add boiling water to the tube to just below the level of the sleeve.

4 Place a small plug of cotton wool in the neck of the tube to prevent heat loss.

5 Measure the temperature as quickly as you can.

6 Read off the temperature every 30 seconds.

7 Plot a graph of the rate of cooling.

There is another way in which heat is lost from the body, which is particularly noticeable on a windy day. If the air can penetrate (that is, blow through) your clothes it can remove heat. That is, heat is transferred by *convection*. Clearly this depends on how easy it is for air to pass through the fabric. A close look at fabric shows that there can be gaps (or *interstices*) for the air to pass through. Figure 7.16 shows this and also shows that in general a knitted fabric (on the right) has bigger gaps than a woven one (on the left).

Once again the difference between fabrics depends on the way they are made. A thick fabric will be better than a thin fabric, and a closely woven fabric will be better than an open one.

Q 10
How could heat loss by convection be stopped?

What you have seen is that staying comfortable (warm or cool) in clothes depends far more on how the fabric and garment are put together than on the fibre from which the clothes are made.

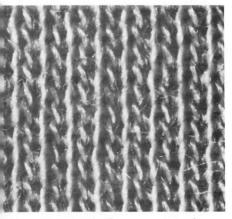

Figure 7.16

7.8
NOTHING IS PERFECT

Q 11

From the results of your tests, compile a chart which shows what aesthetic and performance properties are important for clothes and which of the fibres would give the best results.

Figure 7.17 shows you how to set out your table. (Don't forget flammability.)

Property	Fibre which gives the best performance
water absorption	wool, cotton, and viscose

Figure 7.17

When you have completed your table you will see that no one fibre heads the list in every case.

Remember the third factor affecting choice. Price must not be forgotten. If you look back to Chapter 4 you will see that a fibre like acetate which does not rank top for any performance properties is cheaper than other fibres and so has this advantage. All the fibres are commercially successful to some extent, and therefore each represents a satisfactory solution to the three factors of choice: aesthetics, performance, and price.

THE BEST OF BOTH OR . . .

Since no fibre has the ideal combination of properties it is logical to consider whether using two or more fibres together would give the ideal combination.

This is the idea behind blended fabrics. Examples are polyester/cotton and wool/viscose. The blend is not always made for performance reasons. It may be made for reasons of price and, of course, aesthetics.

Q 12

Write down the names of six blended fabrics that you have heard of. Suggest why these particular blends might have been chosen. (Would it be for aesthetic, performance, or price reasons, or a combination of these three?)

The difficulty is often to know how much of each fibre to use. Clearly a very small percentage of a fibre can have little effect. For example, even though nylon is durable, 2 per cent of it in a viscose fabric will make virtually no difference. Equally, if wool is blended with polyester to give a wool handle, 10 per cent wool is not likely to have any effect. Blends are therefore a compromise. That compromise will not necessarily give everything that is desired. A blend of polyester/cotton cannot be as durable as the same weight fabric in 100 per cent polyester,

Figure 7.18

Figure 7.19
Abrasion tester.

nor can it have the same absorption as the same weight fabric in 100 per cent cotton. It may be, however, an acceptable compromise.

When the composition of a blend is written (as in figure 7.18), the E.E.C. Fibre Content Regulations state that the fibre which is in the largest proportion must be given first and that the percentage of each fibre must be given. So 67/33 polyester/cotton means a blend of polyester and cotton fibres in a fabric, 67 per cent of which is polyester and 33 per cent of which is cotton.

Worksheet FM6 is about thermal insulation and explains the significance of 'tog' ratings. Worksheet FM8 is about the strength of fibres in a woven fabric.

BACKGROUND READING

THEIR TRADE IS RUINING FABRICS
Textile manufacturers have to be sure that their products stand up well to wear and tear — and they have to know this before the cloth is made into clothing and sold to the public. If you buy a shirt which falls apart in a few days it is aggravating for you, infuriating for the shop when you and other dissatisfied customers storm in to complain, and disastrous for the manufacturer when the shop's buyer points out that ten thousand shirts have disintegrated and switches his business to another supplier.

Large clothing buyers — stores such as Marks and Spencer or British Home Stores — set performance standards for the garments they buy. Therefore each type of cloth has to be tested. For the results of the tests to have any meaning, testing must always be done in a repeatable, controlled way by machines of standard design. Textile testing is a surprisingly large business. Each manufacturer has a testing laboratory employing expert technologists and engineers. So do some of the larger buyers. And there are firms whose whole business is making textile testing machinery. One of these is James H. Heal of Halifax, established over 110 years and now employing 50 people.

Heals make devices for measuring properties of fabrics: weight, fibre composition, tensile strength, extensibility (stretch), resistance to abrasion, resistance to 'pilling' (forming of small balls, as on knitwear), permeability to air and water, shrinkage, flammability, colour fastness, seam slippage when pulled, and so on.

Figure 7.19 shows an abrasion tester which tests four samples at once. The upper plate moves in a constantly changing pattern, rubbing the specimens against a standard abrasive material placed on the circular tables of the machine. The weights on top of the vertical rods can be changed — note the tray of spares. In front of that are the windows of counters for the number of rubs. Figure 7.20 shows a standard burning frame for testing flammability. The boxes are controls for a gas flame and timers.

Figure 7.20
Flammability tester.

CHAPTER 8

Building up to a yarn

8.1
SHORT FIBRE TO LONG YARN

The first stage in changing a staple fibre to a fabric is the making of a yarn. The relatively short fibre has to be joined together in some way to produce a yarn of great length which can be used for weaving or knitting. One way might be to glue the fibres together. But the stiffness of the glue means that those necessary aesthetic and performance properties of textiles are lost. However, the fibres can be made to hold together because there is a natural adhesion between them. They will stick together when they are put in contact with each other. Clearly, the more the fibres are in contact the more easily they will hold together.

Q 1
What would be the best way of putting the fibres together to give most contact between individual fibres?

As fibres are not perfectly straight, laying fibres parallel to each other produces a yarn which is thicker than the number of fibres in it. A yarn is quite bulky because air is trapped between the fibres.

You will probably have noticed this in wool which can give bulky fabrics. You saw in section 5.1 that wool fibres are crimped.

HOW IS A YARN BUILT UP FROM A FIBRE?

||| YOU WILL NEED: |||||||||||||||||||||||||||||||||||||||||||||||||||||||||||||||||||||||||||

Wool fibres
or cotton fibres

Tweezers
Hand lens
Ruler

1 Lay the fibres parallel to each other but overlapping, as shown in figure 8.1d.

2 Measure the thickness of the yarn. (Try to get the fibres as close to each other as possible.)

3 Estimate what size you think the yarn would be from the size of the fibres alone.

4 Compare this with the size of the yarn as you have measured it.

Q 2
What is the reason for the difference?

Q 3
Is the yarn strong enough for you to pick up and use?

Figure 8.1

a little contact between the fibres

b maximum contact between the fibres

c yarn would not hold at this point

d fibres must overlap to hold together

e fibres are not straight so bulk is produced due to the air trapped between them

a

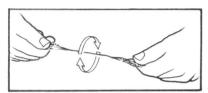

Figure 8.2

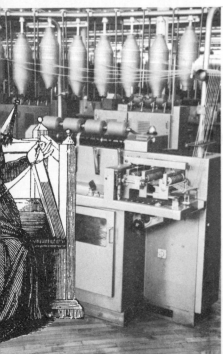

8.2
GIVE IT A TWIST

How then does a textile yarn have enough strength to form part of a fabric? During the yarn making process, *twist* is put into the yarn.

WHAT IS THE EFFECT OF PUTTING TWIST INTO A YARN?

IIII YOU WILL NEED: IIIIIIIIIIIIIIIIIIIIIIIIIIIIIIIIIIIIIIIIIIIIIIIIIIIIIIIIIIIIIIIIIIIIIIIIIIIIIIIIIIIIIII

Wool fibres   Tweezers
or cotton fibres   Hand lens
                                  Ruler

1 Lay the fibres together exactly as you did in section 8.1.

2 Using your fingers, hold the ends of the fibres and twist them together as shown in figure 8.2.

3 While you are twisting the fibres, gently pull the ends of the yarn being made.

Q 4
a What difference do you notice in the thickness of the yarn you have just made, compared with the yarn you made in section 8.1? (You can use a ruler to measure the difference if you wish.)
b Is the yarn stronger than before? Can you now pick it up?

You will have seen that putting twist into the yarn gives it greater strength, and that the more twist there is the stronger the yarn becomes. Twisting increases the amount of surface area of the individual fibres which are in contact with each other. And the more the yarn is twisted the more tightly the fibres are pushed together. The yarn becomes thinner, that is, less bulky.

In production there has to be a compromise. High twist means high strength and low bulk. Low twist means low strength and greater bulk. A less bulky yarn will trap less air and give a thinner fabric. It may be more hard wearing but it will not be such a good insulator.

8.3
COTTON, WOOLLEN, AND WORSTED

The process of producing a yarn from fibres, that is, lining up the fibres and twisting them, is called spinning. From ancient times various methods have been developed for carrying out this process. An early example of how this was done is the distaff spindle. This led to the spinning wheel and finally to modern spinning systems.

Q 5
Look at figure 8.3. How is the lining-up process done in each picture?

Figure 8.3
a *Spinning with the distaff spindle.*
b *Spinning wheel.*
c *Spinning machine which produces worsted yarn.*

In the early processes the lining up was done by hand. That is, the fibres were aligned by hand and then a machine put in the twist. In the modern spinning system, both the aligning of the fibres and the twisting are done by machine. There are three basic spinning systems which have the same principles but which were originally designed for particular natural fibres.

There is the cotton spinning system developed for spinning cotton. There are two systems developed for spinning wool: the woollen system and the worsted system.

The difference between the woollen and worsted systems is related to the connection between fibre alignment, bulk, and twist. Woollen yarns are designed for high bulk. This is done by not aligning the fibres in parallel very much, and giving the yarn relatively low twist. This will give a high bulk yarn.

In the worsted system, the fibres are aligned to a much greater extent and are given a higher twist. This will give a low bulk yarn.

Q 6
Besides bulk, what do you think is likely to be an important difference between woollen and worsted fabrics?

Although the spinning systems were originally designed for natural fibres, man-made fibres are now processed on them, particularly when blends are used. The blending takes place right at the beginning of the yarn-making process so that, for example, polyester and cotton fibres are mixed in the right proportions before spinning and then pass together through the spinning process.

An important point to remember is that a woollen yarn or a worsted yarn does not necessarily mean that the yarn is made from wool. It simply means that whatever fibre is used it has been spun on that particular spinning system.

Worksheet FM7 shows you how to twist wool fleece into a yarn, using a spindle.

8.4
WHAT A WASTE OF TIME!
As you have seen, staple fibres require a considerable amount of processing to convert them into yarn. However, silk and man-made fibres are all produced as filament and are already in yarn form. The spinning system for staple fibres is clearly expensive. It would seem to be a waste of time and money to cut up the filament yarn to staple lengths merely to join it together again by spinning to form a yarn. You can see why this is done when you compare a filament yarn with a spun yarn.

Figure 8.4 shows that what a filament yarn lacks when compared with a spun yarn is bulk. For this reason, filament yarn as produced by a man-made fibre factory is often called flat

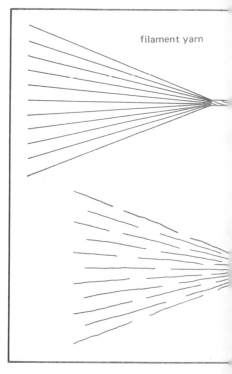

Figure 8.5
Filament yarn and crimped yarn.

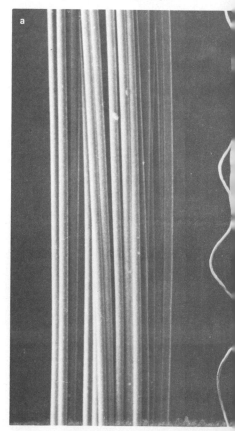

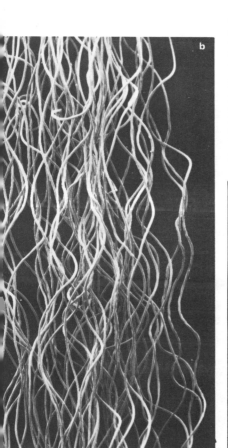

Figure 8.4
Filament yarn and spun yarn.

spun yarn

filament yarn. Of course, some fabrics are made from flat filament yarn. Not surprisingly they are flat, smooth, and thin.

Q 7
Which fabrics made from a natural fibre will be like this?

The aesthetic features described above will be satisfactory for certain end uses, such as ties, linings, shirtings, and some blouse fabrics. For other end uses a bulky yarn is needed. It would be better if flat filament yarn could be given this property without the expense of cutting it up and joining it together again by a staple fibre spinning system. Bulk can be made by the process known as *texturization*. It works this way. Think of a flat filament yarn made up of a number of filaments. Now imagine each of these individual filaments crimped rather like wool fibre is crimped. The result is an increase in bulk, as figure 8.5 shows.

The most popular method of texturizing in commercial production is the *false twist* process. This makes use of one of the properties of synthetic fibres — their ability to be set by heat into a particular shape (see section 7.5). Twist is put into flat filament yarns and set in place by the action of heat. The yarn is cooled and untwisted. As the heat is removed the fibres crimp or 'kink' because of the distortion of the twist previously set in. The yarn is then given a final setting treatment. (See figure 8.6.)

The false-twist method is particularly used for polyester yarn. It came into use commercially, on a large scale, with the introduction by ICI of Crimplene. This was the trade name given to texturized Terylene polyester. There are a large number of other texturizing processes. Although they all give bulk to flat filament yarn, the methods are different and the shape of the final filament varies. An example is the air-jet method often known under the trade name Taslan. This introduces loops into the filaments by blowing a jet of compressed air onto the flat filament yarn. Figure 8.7 on the next page shows how it is done.

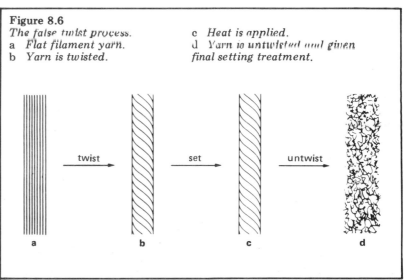

Figure 8.6
The false twist process.
a *Flat filament yarn.*
b *Yarn is twisted.*
c *Heat is applied.*
d *Yarn is untwisted and given final setting treatment.*

twist → set → untwist

a   b   c   d

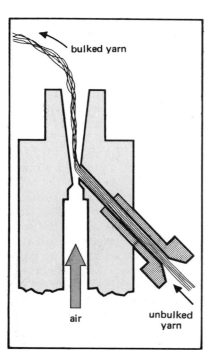

Figure 8.7
The air-jet texturizing method.

8.5
FLAT AND TEXTURIZED FILAMENT YARNS AND SPUN YARNS

First look at the difference between flat and texturized filament yarns.

|||| YOU WILL NEED: |||||||||||||||||||||||||||||||||||||||||||||||||||||||||||||||||||||||||||
Sample of flat filament yarn on a piece of card
Sample of false twist yarn on a piece of card

Hand lens
Ruler

1 Look at the sample yarns under the hand lens and record their appearance on the card. (Are they flat or crimped?)

2 Measure the length of the yarns. Record the length on the card.

3 Stretch the yarns and measure them again. Record the length.

4 Allow the yarns to relax and measure them again. Record this length too.

Q 8
Which yarn can be stretched more?

Q 9
Which of the two yarns recovers better from stretching?

Q 10
Which of the two yarns is more bulky?

AESTHETICS AGAIN

You have seen that texturization can give bulk to a flat filament yarn so that it seems like a spun yarn. But is it? The real test must come when the yarns are converted into fabrics. Does a fabric made from spun yarn produced from staple fibres have the same aesthetics as a fabric made in the same way but from texturized filament yarn?

Q 11
What factors must be the same to make the comparison a scientific one?

Now compare fabrics of similar weight made from texturized and spun polyester.

|||| YOU WILL NEED: |||||||||||||||||||||||||||||||||||||||||||||||||||||||||||||||||||||||||||||||||||
Sample of woven texturized filament polyester
Sample of woven spun staple fibre polyester

Examine the two sample fabrics and compare them for handle, drape, and appearance, in the same way as you did in section 7.3.

Q 12
What differences do you notice? Which do you prefer?

8.6
FANCY AND EXOTIC

So far the yarns you have looked at have been simple yarns, that is, they have been even and have had the same appearance throughout. Ply yarns are composed of two or more simple yarns twisted or 'plied' together.

If two simple yarns are used then two-ply yarn is formed. If three yarns are used three-ply yarn is formed, and so on. Ply yarns give a slightly different aesthetic appearance from single yarns. *Complex* or *novelty* yarns differ from simple yarns in that their structure varies along the length of the yarn in size, twist, and effect. Complex yarns usually have two or more plies, one ply being the base or core, another ply giving the effect, and a third holding them together.

As an example, bouclé yarns have loops sticking out from the main part of the yarn, and knop or knot yarns have thick segments at intervals along the yarn.

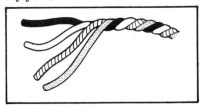

Figure 8.8
Ply yarn.

EXAMINING FANCY YARN STRUCTURE

||| YOU WILL NEED: ||||||||||||||||||||||||||||||||||||||||||||||||||||||||||||||||||||||||||||||||||||||||||||||||||||

Samples of bouclé, knop, two-ply yarns

Hand lens
Dissecting needle

1 Examine the yarn samples under the hand lens.

2 Separate the plies using the dissecting needle.

3 Identify the core ply and the effect ply in the complex yarns.

Q 13

a How have texture and appearance been obtained for each yarn?

b How might this affect their performance and cost?

BACKGROUND READING

THE TECHNICAL MANAGER

Bob Jones is the Technical Manager of a yarn manufacturer. He is responsible for the quality of the yarns produced. The yarn is sold to weavers and knitters who produce a wide variety of textile items. The production of synthetic yarns requires rigorous monitoring. This ensures that they are consistent as a product in terms of evenness and feel. Yarns must also take up dye uniformly so that finished garments will be of a level shade — sleeves must match!

The Technical Manager works closely with production managers and is in charge of the Quality Laboratory. In the laboratory he has two technologists and five laboratory assistants, including Ann Saunders and Dick Rushton who are both seventeen and in their first jobs. Bob believes that every member of staff should not only know the correct method for carrying out a test but they should also be aware of why each test is carried out. It is

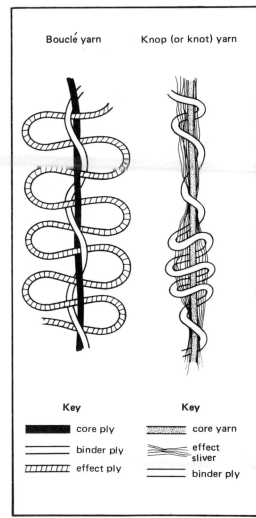

Boucle yarn   Knop (or knot) yarn

Key		Key	
▬ core ply		░░░ core yarn	
── binder ply		✕ effect sliver	
⊓⊓⊓ effect ply		── binder ply	

Figure 8.9
Two complex yarns.

also important that they know what effect an 'out-of-line' test result could have on the final yarn and the garment made from it.

Checking the quality of production covers the whole operation from raw material supplied in containers to yarn dispatched to manufacturers. All the staff in the laboratory must be very careful in the way each test is carried out and the results meticulously recorded.

The raw material arrives at the mill in 10-tonne containers. Samples of this are regularly taken for testing. These tests indicate molecular weight which affects durability, extensibility, and dye affinity. Ann has been working in this part of the laboratory since she arrived and has reached the stage when all of her results are not automatically checked by someone else.

Once a batch of raw material has been checked for quality (within hours of arrival), it is released for production. Further checks during production make sure that the extrusion process has not affected dyeability and that the thickness of the fibre strands is correct.

Yarn is purchased by weavers and knitters as the raw material to make into fabrics or garments. The yarn manufacturer has to check that both the yarn and the garments made from it will meet certain standards. Checks are made on the main yarn properties such as thickness and extensibility. The actual test will depend on whether the yarn is made of a continous filament or a staple type fibre.

Yarns are also knitted and woven into fabric samples for fabric performance tests. Dick Rushton has been working on this type of check for nearly twelve months. His work consists of machine knitting samples of fabric from yarn and testing them. This includes abrasion testing for wear, washing tests for shrinkage, and sample dyeing for uniformity of dye uptake.

Bob Jones, as Technical Manager, also visits the factories he supplies to deal with enquiries. The laboratory will investigate any complaints, not only to satisfy the customer, but also to find the cause of any fault so that action can be taken.

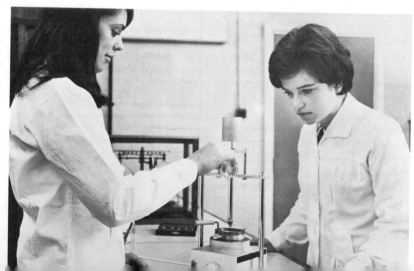

Figure 8.10

CHAPTER 9
Building up to a fabric

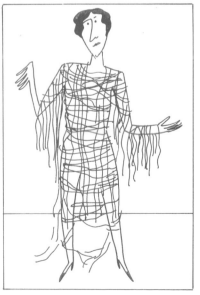

Figure 9.1

Figure 9.2
Maori dancers.

9.1
YARN TO FABRIC

The first stage in converting fibre to fabric is the production of the yarn. However, this would be of limited use in covering the human body. Yarns alone would not hold together because they are in effect a single dimension. A yarn could be draped over the length of the body but it would not hold together in the width. If the yarns were somehow draped across the width of the body they would never hold together in the length.

The only way a type of yarn could be used for clothing would be as in the example of a grass skirt which is only acceptable because it is very thick, or because other clothes are worn.

Therefore, it is obvious that if the one-dimensional yarn is to be successfully used for clothing it must be changed into a two-dimensional form. This is the process of fabric manufacture.

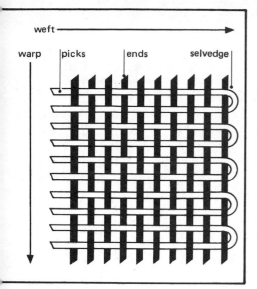

weft →

warp | picks | ends | selvedge

Figure 9.4

Figure 9.5

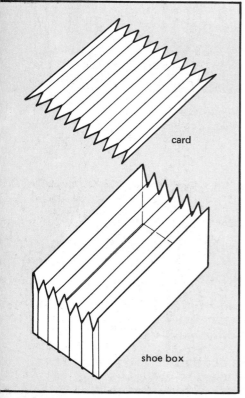

card

shoe box

Figure 9.3
Linen cloth used for bandaging mummies, and two spindles

9.2
INTERLACING

The basic problem to be solved in fabric manufacture is to find a way to hold together yarns so that they lie in both directions, that is both horizontally and vertically. The oldest way of doing this is by weaving. Woven fabrics have been found in the tombs of Ancient Egypt, where woven cloth was used to wrap the bodies before they were put in the tombs.

Weaving solves the problem of holding yarns in two dimensions by *interlacing* the yarns at right angles to each other. By varying the interlacing sequence, different patterns can be produced. In woven fabrics the yarns that run down the length of the fabric are called *warp* yarns or *ends*. Those which run across the width of the fabric are called *weft* yarns or *picks*. See figure 9.4.

The edges of the fabric are woven in a particular way to stop the yarns slipping out. These edges are called the *selvedge*.

HOW IS A WEAVE PATTERN PRODUCED?

||| YOU WILL NEED: ||||||||||||||||||||||||||||||||||||||||||||||||||||||||||||||||||

Yarn samples for weaving   Hand lens
4 fabric samples to copy   Old shoe box or card
                                  Bodkin (large)

1 Shape the shoe box or card so that it forms a basic weaving loom. Figure 9.5 shows you how to do this.

2 Tie lengths of yarn down the length of the box or card. These are your warp threads.

3 Take a length of yarn and thread one end through the bodkin. The yarn is your weft thread.

4 Weave the weft thread across the warp threads so that you make a *plain* weave pattern. To do this the first row should be *over* one warp thread *under* one warp thread. The second row is

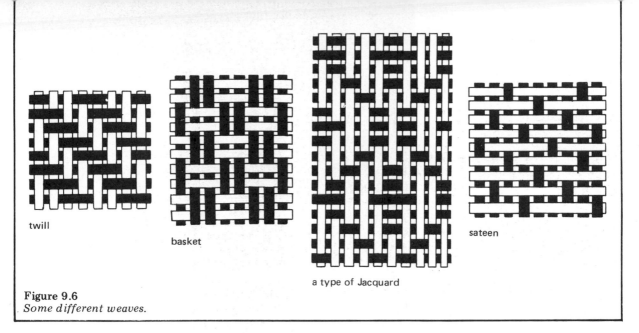

twill

basket

a type of Jacquard

sateen

Figure 9.6
Some different weaves.

the reverse, that is *under* one warp thread *over* one warp thread. Repeat this pattern for six rows. You have now made a simple piece of fabric like the one in figure 9.7.

5 Look at the fabric samples you have been given under the hand lens. Look at the way the pattern has been formed. With your weaving loom and thread try to copy the pattern you can see. You may need to use different coloured threads in the warp and weft to get the right result.

You could also try to interlace the yarns to make the weaves shown in figure 9.6 (above).

The experiments with weaving give you some idea of the range of patterns which can be produced, but this is only one aspect of the variety that can be introduced into weaving. If yarns of different size are used, fabric weight and thickness can be altered. Variations can also happen because of what is known as *tightness of construction* or *sett*, that is, how closely the yarns are packed together in both the warp and weft directions. So by varying the yarn count, the tightness of construction, and the pattern of interlacing a vast range of fabrics is produced.

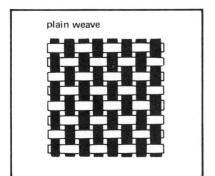

plain weave

Figure 9.7

Figure 9.8
Slippage.

The construction affects the properties of the fabric. You know that a thick heavy fabric will have better durability than a thin light fabric, if they are made from the same fibre. If the yarns are too widely spaced the fabric will not hold together. Remember that the fabric holds together because of the friction at the points of contact of the interlacing yarns. If the construction is too loose the yarns slip over one another and the fabric falls apart.

Q 1
Where on a garment might you expect slippage to be a problem?

You can investigate how the structure of a fabric affects its strength, using worksheet FM8.

Figure 9.9
A warping machine. This builds up the warp on a beam which is then transferred to the loom.

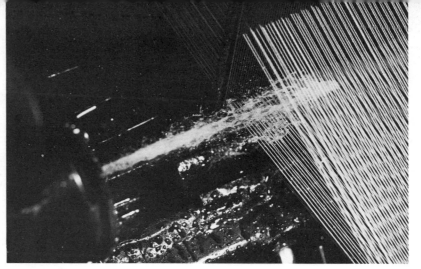

Figure 9.10
The weft can be carried across in a water jet.

Figure 9.11
In the textile industry, modern automatic weaving machines operate without shuttles. In the craft sector, and for experimenting with new designs on a small scale, older looms with shuttles like this are still in use.

9.3
THE LOOM

In industry, weaving is carried out on a loom. The earliest looms were operated by hand, but during the Industrial Revolution mechanization was introduced so looms became machine powered. But they work on the same principle of interlacing as the weaving you did in section 9.2.

9.4
LOCKING LOOPS

Another method which can be used to hold yarns in two-dimensional structures to form a fabric is to form the yarn into rows of interlocking loops like the one in figure 9.14.

A loop means that the yarn is lying in both horizontal and vertical directions so that interlocking them produces the two-dimensional form required. This is *knitting*. There are two types of knitting. In the first the fabric is made by forming loops from the yarn across the width or around a circle. This is called *weft-knitting*.

In the second method the loops are formed in a vertical direction, and the fabric holds together by interlocking these vertical loops with the loops on alternate sides. This is called *warp-knitting*.

There are many pattern possibilities in both weft- and warp-knitting. As with weaving, the weight of the fabric, and hence its properties, are affected by the yarn used and the tightness of construction. Some of the common weft-knitted fabrics are jersey made from cotton, wool, acrylic, and texturized polyester yarns. Another common form of weft-knitting is what is often termed 'knitwear', such as fully-fashioned sweaters and, of course, hand knitting. A great deal of warp-knitted fabric is made from flat filament nylon yarn and is used for underwear and lingerie, and sometimes for sheets, shirtings, and blouse fabrics.

Figure 9.12
Weft-knitting machine.

Figure 9.13
Warp-knitting machine.

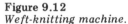

Figure 9.14

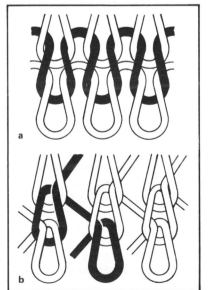

Figure 9.15
a *Weft-knitting.*
b *Warp-knitting.*

HOW IS A KNITTED FABRIC CONSTRUCTED?

⦚ YOU WILL NEED: ⦚⦚

Knitting wool
2 knitting needles

1 Ask your teacher for help if you have never knitted before.

2 Cast on 20 stitches.

3 Knit 10 rows using plain stitch only.

What you have done by hand has to be speeded up in industry by machines like the ones in figures 9.12 and 9.13.

9.5
STRETCH

There are many aesthetic differences between weft- and warp-knitted fabrics and woven fabrics. Different pattern effects are obtainable. There are also differences in production costs. Weaving is generally slower than either weft or warp-knitting although modern looms are reducing this gap. This cost factor must be balanced against differences in aesthetics and performance.

Although properties such as durability and washing performance depend very much on the fibre used and the weight of the fabric, there is an important difference between woven and knitted fabrics. This relates to the question of stretch. As you know, the body bends at the elbows, knees, across the shoulders, and so on. Clearly, if clothing restricted this movement it would be very uncomfortable to wear. If the fabric could stretch it might be an advantage.

Figure 9.16

1 *Measure the length of the fabric sample.*

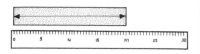

2 *Hold each end of the sample in your hands. Pull outwards so that the maximum stretch is obtained.*

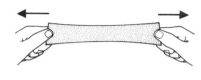

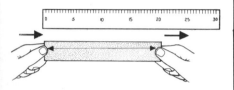

3 *Measure the new length. Release the fabric and allow it to recover for 10 minutes.*

4 *Measure the fabric strips again.*

COMPARING STRETCH

Compare the stretch of weft- and warp-knitted and woven fabrics on the straight and on the bias.

||| YOU WILL NEED: ||||||||||||||||||||||||||||||||||||||||||||||||||||||||||||||||||||||||

Samples of fabrics (3 cm × 20 cm)
Metre rule

1 Measure the length of the fabric sample (see figure 9.16).

2 Hold each end of the sample in your hands. Pull outwards so that the maximum stretch is obtained.

3 Measure the new length. Release the fabric and allow it to recover for 10 minutes.

4 Measure the fabric strips again.

Q 2

Which fabric gave the greatest amount of stretch?

Q 3

Can you relate the amount of stretch to the types of garments usually made from the fabrics?

5 Do the same thing again, but this time using fabric samples which have been cut on the bias.

Q 4

What are the main differences that you have found? Record your answers.

9.6
MISSING OUT THE YARN

The processes of knitting and weaving have been designed to convert the one-dimensional yarn into a two-dimensional fabric. However, a two-dimensional form can be produced from fibres simply by laying them in a random form, in the shape of a flat sheet or web. The question is, how can this web be held together?

Various solutions to this problem have been tried. Because they all convert the fibre into a fabric without going first to a yarn or using the conventional techniques of weaving or knitting, the fibres produced are often called *nonwovens*.

STICKING THE WEB

One obvious way of holding the web together would be an adhesive (or glue). The web is coated with an adhesive which is then dried and cured. These nonwoven fabrics are known as *bonded-fibre* fabrics. A common brand name for them is Vilene.

STITCHING THE WEB

Another method which has been used to hold the web together is to stitch it. These fabrics are often called *stitch-bonded*.

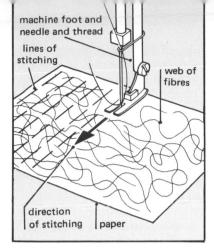

machine foot and
needle and thread

lines of
stitching

web of
fibres

direction
of stitching | paper

Figure 9.17

Figure 9.18
Stitch-bonded fabric.

HOW IS A STITCH-BONDED FABRIC MADE?

IIII YOU WILL NEED: IIIIIIIIIIIIIIIIIIIIIIIIIIIIIIIIIIIIIIIIIIIIIIIIIIIIIIIIIIIIIIIIII
Thread (spun polyester)
Polyester fibre
Sheet of paper
Sewing machine

1 Lay the fibres on a sheet of paper to form a fibre web.

2 Put the fibre and paper under the needle of the machine and sew a straight line through both materials.

3 Continue doing this until the fibres are held in place by the stitching. (See figure 9.17.)

4 When you have finished stitching, remove the paper.

5 Test the fabric you have made by rubbing it and pulling it.

Q 5
Do you think your fabric will have any performance weaknesses? If so, what will they be?

9.7
AESTHETICS YET AGAIN
Nonwoven fabrics made by cutting out the yarn stage are often cheaper, but as always it is necessary to consider if the aesthetics and performance are satisfactory.

COMPARING WOVEN AND NONWOVEN FABRICS

IIII YOU WILL NEED: IIIIIIIIIIIIIIIIIIIIIIIIIIIIIIIIIIIIIIIIIIIIIIIIIIIIIIIIIIIIIIIIIIIIIIIIIIIIIIIIIIIIIIIIIIIIII
Samples of woven and nonwoven fabrics

Examine the fabrics and compare them for handle, drape, and appearance. (See section 7.3.)

Q 6
What purpose could the nonwoven fabrics serve in garments?

Q 7
What common household textile item could be and often is made from nonwoven fabrics?

Q 8
Why is a nonwoven fabric suitable for this purpose?

BACKGROUND READING

THE WEAVER AS HE USED TO BE
About three hundred years ago, someone wrote the song of 'The Jolly Weaver':

> *If it was not for the weavers, our backs would all go bare*
> *If it wasn't for the work of the weavers.*

In those days looms were very simple, and a weaver would work in his own home. He would buy yarn, weave it, and sell the cloth; or perhaps a merchant would do the buying and selling, and pay the weaver for his work. If your surname is Weaver or Webster, probably one of your ancestors followed this trade.

A man might farm as well as weave. Richard Lansdale, who lived in a village called Eccles, in Lancashire, died in 1588, the year of the Spanish Armada. We still have the list of property he left: a loom and two spinning wheels, a valuable stock of yarn (worth nearly £20, a lot of money then), and two cows, three horses, and two pigs, besides poultry and some growing crops. Lansdale's possessions were worth about £84, so he was quite well off. A poorer weaver, John Turnough, of Oldham, died in 1592. He left possessions worth only £8 15s (£8.75), and most of this was his loom, worth £1 8s, and cloth he had woven, worth £4 6s 8d. He doesn't seem to have farmed.

Changes soon came. In 1733 John Kay invented the 'flying shuttle'. The weaver jerked this shuttle through the loom so much faster than he could throw it by hand that he could make at least twice as much cloth — and money — every day. In the 1760s such men as the famous Richard Arkwright developed machinery to make yarn. Until then, it had all been made by women using spinning wheels.

Figure 9.19
Power loom weaving in 1835.

Now weavers of fine cloths often made plenty of money. In the words of a Bolton man of the 1790s, 'Weavers were vastly well off. . . . They wore top boots and ruffled shirts, carried a cane, and sometimes travelled by coach.' But the weavers making the cheaper cloths were still desperately poor: 'They are clothed in rags. . . . Their labour is excessive, not infrequently 16 hours a day. . . .'

A much greater change was on its way. Before 1800 power-driven looms had been invented, and by about 1830 the place for a weaver was in a factory, tending steam-powered looms. He had to fit in with the factory routine:

In the morning just at six o'clock the engine will begin,
And you must set off running for to work you must be in.
For should it happen that you be ten minutes there too late
You must give in your number and twopence they will take.

On the other hand, the factory owners often built good small houses for their workers, together with shops, chapels, pubs, and sometimes schools. Girls, too, found that they could earn good wages by working in the factories:

I am a hand weaver to my trade
But I fell in love with a factory maid,
And if I could her favour win
I'd stand by her and weave by steam.

Some things don't seem to have changed, even if the job has.

CHAPTER 10
Colour

10.1
SUBTRACTION

When you think of light you usually think of white light, but as you know it is made up from a number of colours.

Q 1

Where in nature can you easily see white light split up into colours?

If you could remove one or more of the individual colours, what remained would be a mixture of the rest of the colours. If you removed red, you would be left with a blue—green colour. In the same way if you removed either violet or blue you would be left with a mixture of colours but more yellow or yellow—green than before.

Now suppose you could remove all the colours except red.

Q 2

What colour do you think the object would appear this time?

This is what has happened when you look at something red. A substance in the thing you see has removed or *absorbed* part of the white light that shines on it. What is reflected back is what you can see. In the case of a red object, this is just the red light.

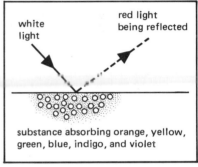

substance absorbing orange, yellow, green, blue, indigo, and violet

Figure 10.1

Q 3

Suppose the object on which white light shone absorbed red, orange, yellow, green, indigo, and violet. What colour would you see the object as being?

Q 4

What colour would the object be if it did not absorb any white light?

Q 5

What colour would the object be if it absorbed all the white light?

(Worksheet FM9 shows you how to break up white light into its different colours.)

ROSES ARE RED, VIOLETS ARE BLUE

Now you can understand why the eye sees different colours. In the dark everything appears black but when there is light some substances can absorb parts of the visible light. That is, they can absorb some of the colours which make up white light and reflect back others. Your eye sees the colours which are reflected back.

Roses are red because in the petals are chemicals, sometimes called *pigments*, which absorb most of the colours of the spectrum except the red. This is reflected back, so it looks red.

Q 6
What does this mean for a white rose?

10.2
DYES

Colour has an aesthetic appeal to everybody. The chances are that your ideas will be different from your friends, but remember that when you were asked in Chapter 1 why you chose a particular dress or shirt you may well have said 'Because I liked the colour'.

Everybody has definite likes and dislikes about colours. When you buy your clothes or choose a colour scheme for your room, you expect to be able to choose from a vast range of colours.

Nearly all fibres are white or creamy when they are first produced. So for the great range of colours needed in fashion, something must be added to the fibres. Whatever is added must do more than just give the right colours. It would be quite useless if all the colour in your clothes faded or rubbed off when you wore them, or if they washed out the first time you cleaned them. The substance added must stay in the fabric. That is, it must be *fast*.

Dyestuffs are chemical substances which have to be made fast or bonded in some way to the textile fibre. How do different fibres react to a dye?

DYEING COTTON AND POLYESTER FABRICS

IIII **YOU WILL NEED:** IIIIIIIIIIIIIIIIIIIIIIIIIIIIIIIIIIIIIIIIIIIIIIIIIIIIIIIIIIIIIIIIIIIIIIIIIIIIIIIIII

Cotton fabric, 2 20-cm squares	Scissors
Polyester fabric, 2 20-cm squares	Kettle or saucepan
Dyestuff	Washing-up bowl
Salt	Jug
Washing powder, 1 15-ml	Spoon for mixing
(table) spoon	Rubber gloves
	Skewer

1 Mark the cotton fabric with scissor cuts.

2 To get the best results from the dye, first read the manufacturer's instructions carefully.

3 Following the instructions, dye one piece of the cotton fabric and one piece of the polyester fabric, putting them in the solution at the same time.

4 Look at the results of dyeing the cotton and the polyester fabric.

Figure 10.2

Q 7

Was all the dye transferred to the fabrics, or was some left in the dye solution?

Q 8

Did the cotton fabric seem to take up the dye easily?

Q 9

Is there any difference in the depth of colour you got on the cotton fabric and the polyester fabric?

Q 10

Is the dye fast on both fabrics? (Test this by washing each sample in hand-hot water using washing powder.)

Q 11

Is the dye you used good for both cotton and polyester?

Q 12

Can you think of any reason why this is so? (Look back to the structure of fibres in Chapter 5 for a clue.)

Some dyes work on polyester, some on cotton. For the best results you need to know what the fabric is made of and whether the dye is suitable for it.

Years ago the only dyestuffs available were those from natural sources, mainly animals and vegetables. You might be surprised to know that fabrics over three and a half thousand years old have been found with remains of indigo dyestuff in them. One of the most remarkable dyes used in the ancient world was produced from a tiny snail, found near the city of Tyre in the Mediterranean. About 12 000 snails were needed to make 1 gram of dyestuff, but the colour obtained was a beautiful purple. Because it was so expensive to produce, it was only available to the wealthy, which is why purple is thought of as a 'royal' colour.

In 1856 William Perkin made the first synthetic dyestuff. This discovery started the modern dyestuff industry. Today nearly all dyes are made synthetically and thousands are available to the textile industry. Dyestuffs are generally divided up into classes. Each class is related chemically and tends to be used for a particular type of fibre.

Use worksheets FM10, FM11, and FM12 to find the effectiveness of different dyes and how they withstand light, washing, and dry cleaning.

10.3
FINGERPRINTS

So far you have only looked at the primary colours. You may have wondered how so many shades and tints of colours are made. You know that a dye absorbs some colours of the spectrum. But the dye does not absorb each colour in the same

75

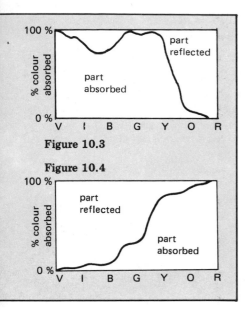

Figure 10.3

Figure 10.4

amount. One dye might absorb all the red, some of the orange, and a little of the green. The colour reflected back which you see is a subtle mixture of the remaining colours.

You can show this on a graph. This is called the *absorption spectrum* of the dye. Every dye has its own absorption spectrum like its own individual fingerprint.

Q 13
If you used a dye with the absorption spectrum shown in figure 10.3, what sort of colour do you think it would give?

You can now see how some shades and tints are made.

Q 14
How do you think the range of colours can be made bigger still?

Colours on fabrics are not always made by using only one dyestuff. Two or even more dyes can be used. The absorption spectrum of each of the dyes joins to give the overall colour effect.

Q 15
What colour would you see if the dyes with the absorption spectra shown in figures 10.3 and 10.4 were used together?

Worksheet FM13 shows you how to achieve colour tints by mixing dyes.

BACKGROUND READING

THE USE OF COLOUR
We all have our favourite colours and colour schemes, in much the same way that we each like different types of music, and it is this as well as pattern that usually governs our choice when we buy a garment or fabric to decorate a room. But despite our personal likes and dislikes, colours also have the property of evoking in us different moods and feelings. There are warm colours, such as red, brown, and orange, or cold colours like shades of blue and grey. Then, one hears many other descriptions of colours and their combinations, such as cheerful, drab, harmonious, or harsh.

When using colour, the main consideration is always: what will the fabric be used for? and with dress fabrics: for which season is it intended? This is important as often our choice of colours reflects a particular season, and also the fact that dark colours absorb heat and so are worn in winter, whereas light colours reflect heat and are useful for the summer months.

When choosing colours for furnishing fabrics there are many further considerations, such as the moods one wishes to create in a particular room. Will the fabric blend with the other furnishings? Is it suitable for the function of a room? And especially important in wallpaper design where a large area is

covered: will it be too dominant and detract from all other furnishings in the room? It is for these reasons as well as personal preferences that most fabrics are produced in a variety of different colourways. It may be possible to buy one design in soft pastel shades for use in a bedroom or in warmer tones for use in a living-room.

Regarding the actual use of colour when designing fabrics, there are no set rules, since much of the choice is dictated by the preference of a particular firm or even country. A definite colour mood can be created by using different shades of one colour, or a predominance of one colour. The design could have a light cream background, to blend with the image and create a soft overall tone. Or it could have a dark background such as dark green, brown, or black that would give more emphasis to the lighter colours of the image, in much the same way as in nature one sees the sun illuminating trees or birds against a dark storm cloud.

Another important factor is that the cost of the fabric increases according to the number of colours used, and part of the art of designing includes producing an effective design with a minimum number of colours. The number used in a design varies from one or two up to about eighteen colours.

You will read about the work of one designer in the Background reading to the next chapter. He finds great enjoyment in observing colour in nature and creating different moods by applying them to fabric; from the intensity of spring, through the mellow richness of summer to the more sombre browns, golds, and greys of autumn and winter. Or just the variety of shades on the bark of a tree during the changing light of a single day.

Figure 10.5
The colour scheme in this room makes it look light and larger than it is.

CHAPTER 11

Putting colour into practice

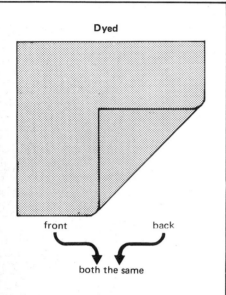

Dyed

front   back

both the same

Printed

front   back

different

Figure 11.1
The difference between a dyed and printed fabric.

Figure 11.2
a *Package dyeing machine.*
b *Polyester fabric which has been dyed under pressure in a jet dyeing machine.*

11.1
COMMERCIAL PRACTICE

You know that dyes are used to get colour into textiles. To do this the dyer in a textile works has many problems to solve. He or she must get the right colour. This may mean matching colours on two different fabrics, and making sure that the colour is *fast*. The fabric must not be damaged during dyeing. It must be dyed evenly. Dyeing and dyestuffs are expensive, and the cost must be kept as low as possible.

The basic method of dyeing is nearly always the same. The dye is dissolved or suspended as very fine particles in water. The textile is then immersed in it. A few dyes can work in cold solutions by immersing for a very short time. Most dyes need heat over a length of time which may sometimes be many hours. Some classes of dyestuff need pressure to work. This means that many different types of machines are used for dyeing, and these vary according to whether it is the fabric, the yarn, or the fibre which is being dyed.

When you dye a textile the whole of it is immersed in the dye. This means that if you do it correctly the colour will be the same from all angles and from both sides. You can also apply colour to one surface, that is one side only, of a textile. This is called *printing*. The same dyes are used for both processes, but after printing you need an extra treatment to make the dye fast.

Colouring fabrics by dyeing or printing means that a vast range of pattern and colour effects can be made. You can now think about how this is done.

a

11.2
ALL THOSE PATTERNS

When you think about dyeing you probably think first about fabric dyeing. That is, you take a completed fabric where the fibres have been spun and formed into yarn. The yarn has been woven or knitted to make a fabric, and then you colour it. However, there is no reason why this should be the only way.

Q 1
At what other stages in the textile chain do you think colour could be applied?

If you took fibres, dyed them different colours, mixed them together, and then spun a yarn you would have a *mixture yarn*. Now suppose you weave different mixture yarns to make a fabric. This is how the many varied patterns of tweed are made.

Instead of dyeing the fibres, you could dye the yarn. Each yarn would be a different colour.

Q 2
How do you think a woven check fabric is made?

Gingham and the sort of checks used on shirts and blouses are fairly simple designs made in weaving, but some looms can make very complicated patterns. They have complex mechanisms for choosing different yarns at different times. This system was invented by a Frenchman, Joseph-Marie Jacquard. These give very complex patterns often used for towels or furnishings.

Differently-coloured yarns are also used in knitting. A Jacquard mechanism can be attached to a jersey machine to give very complex patterns.

Finally, as you know, the fabric alone can be dyed. This is sometimes called *piece* dyeing. In most cases this gives an even plain colour over the whole fabric. However, suppose you made up a fabric using two fibres. One fibre took up the dyestuff and the other fibre did not.

b

Figure 11.3
A sample of Harris tweed.

Figure 11.4
A woven checked shirt.

Figure 11.5
Jacquard fabric can be used for aeroplane seats

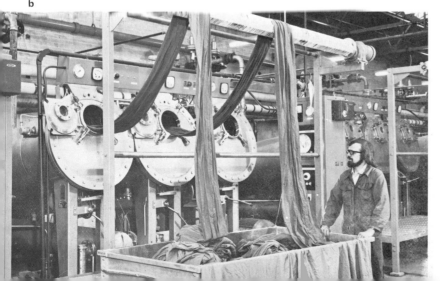

Q 3

What do you think the result would be if you piece-dyed this fabric?

This process is often used for fabrics made from nylon and polyester. The nylon and polyester are woven or knitted to make the fabric in such a way that when the fabric is dyed using a class of dye which adheres to nylon, a pattern is produced. This is because the nylon takes up the dye and the polyester does not. This process is called *cross dyeing*. Look back at figure 1.6 which shows a cross-dyed sock.

EXAMINING FABRICS TO FIND THE DYEING STAGES

||||| YOU WILL NEED: |||||||||||||||||||||||||||||||||||||||||||||||||||||||||||||||||||||||||||||||

Fabric samples

Dissecting needle
Hand lens

1 Take one fabric sample and examine it with the hand lens. Use the dissecting needle to separate the fibres if you need to.

2 Repeat the process for each sample you have been given.

Q 4

At which stage of the textile chain was the fabric sample dyed? Was it:
a the fibre stage
b the yarn stage
c the fabric stage?

You can see that all these methods are used for commercial fabrics, but they will vary in cost.

Q 5

Which do you think would cost less to dye, a plain single colour or a check produced by yarn dyeing?

11.3
ROLLERS: CHEAP AND SIMPLE

You have probably done some form of printing yourselves such as lino or potato printing. This is the easiest way to print. The colour is put on from a block. The design is prepared on the block by cutting away the background so the design area is raised. Dye is applied to the surface of the block and the block is laid on the fabric. The process obviously takes a long time. Samples of fabrics with block prints have been found from as early as 1600 B.C.

Q 6

Why does block printing take a long time?

You will know that the two main problems with block printing are that you can only cover a small area of the fabric at one time and that you need a different block for each colour. This method is too slow for industry, so it has to be automated. A simple idea is used. The block is made into a roller. This over-

Figure 11.6
Potato printing.

comes the first problem, because as the roller turns the fabric moves continuously under it. However, you still need a different roller for each colour. This method is called *roller printing*. The design is built up from several rollers, each applying a different colour, and working fast and continuously. It has been in use for many years and is the cheapest form of printing.

Although relatively cheap, this method is not very good for giving fine detail. For aesthetic reasons, there is room for a better printing method.

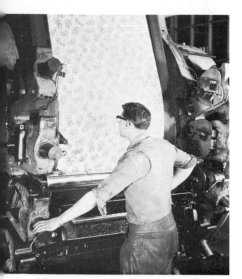

Figure 11.7
Roller printing machine.

11.4
SCREENS: EXPENSIVE AND COMPLICATED
You have probably made patterns using a stencil. Stencil printing was first developed by the Japanese. The same principle is applied to screen printing.

You can make a screen by covering a frame with a fine fabric such as silk or nylon. A film with the design cut out is laid on the screen. This then works in the same way as a stencil, that is, the dyestuff can only pass through the parts of the fine mesh screen left open, and so a pattern is printed on the fabric underneath.

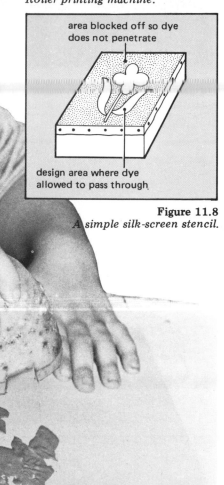

Figure 11.8
A simple silk-screen stencil.

area blocked off so dye does not penetrate

design area where dye allowed to pass through

To print, you place the screen on the fabric with the design still facing downwards. Add the dye at one edge of the frame and use a rubber knife or squeegee to move the dye across the screen and force the dye through the open areas of the mesh onto the fabric. You can see that, like hand block printing, the process is slow and also needs one screen per colour. However, you can get fine detail. Automatic flat screen printing has been used for many years. The screens are placed on the fabric automatically, in order, but it is still a relatively slow process (approximately 6 metres of fabric are printed per minute). This compares with roller printing where as much as 50 metres can be printed per minute.

Q 7
How could screen printing be speeded up?

Even with a rotary screen you can still only use one screen per colour, but the process is now continuous. Rotary screen printing can be as fast as roller printing. The screens are cheaper than rollers to produce, but they do not last as long.

11.5
ANOTHER WAY
When you carry out dyeing and printing the dyestuffs are usually in a solution with water. The water helps the dye to penetrate into the fabric. You know that there are sometimes difficulties in transferring the dye into the fabric. This is why dyes are sometimes not fast. Therefore long processing times are sometimes needed to get good results.

Suppose the dye were in the form of a *vapour* or *gas*. The molecules of the dye could then penetrate into the fibre more easily and the process be finished in a short time. This is the principle behind the newest method of printing, called *transfer printing*.

The design is printed onto paper. This can be done easily and cheaply in a variety of colours because paper printing is a relatively cheap process. The dyes used are called *disperse* dyes, the same types as are used for dyeing polyester fibres. The paper is laid against the fabric and heat is applied. The dye changes from a solid on the paper to a vapour which changes again into a solid on the fabric. This is called *sublimation*. The dye in vapour form has little or no attraction for the paper but a high attraction for certain textile fibres, particularly polyester. The dye penetrates the fibre, the colour is set in, and the print is transferred. This process is very fast. The principle is used for applying motifs to garments or printing complete rolls of fabrics.

Transfer printing from paper to fabric is slower than roller printing (20 metres per minute) but transfer printing paper is cheap and the process has many advantages. There is no need for extra setting processes to make the dye fast. As no water is used there is no problem of liquid waste disposal. It works very well on polyester but also on other fibres and is rapidly becoming one of the most important printing processes.

Figure 11.9
Transfer printing machine.

Figure 11.10
The inspiration.

TRANSFER PRINTING
How does transfer printing work? What are the results like?

|||| YOU WILL NEED: ||||||||||||||||||||||||||||||||||||||||||||||||||||||||||||||||||||||||||||||||||

Transfer printing paper
Polyester fabric
15-ml (table) spoon washing powder

Clock or watch with seconds hand
Iron pre-heated to its highest setting
Ironing board
Washing-up bowl

1 Put the polyester fabric onto the ironing board and cover it with the transfer printing paper.

2 Make sure the printed side of the paper is against the fabric.

3 Using the preheated iron, press the paper for approximately 15 seconds. Do not move the iron over the paper. Take care that the iron does not come into contact with the ⚠ polyester fabric.

4 Remove the iron and paper and observe the print.

5 Cut the printed sample in half.

6 Wash one half of the sample in hand hot water and washing powder to test the fastness of the dye.

Q 8
Was the transfer print fast or did the colours run?

Q 9
Was the print sharp?

DESIGNING FABRICS

All the printed fabrics that you wear or have in your home have been designed by someone. Philip Jacobs is a professional artist and designer of fabrics, wallpapers, household linens, and plates. Here is his description of how he works.

Before I start designing a collection of fabrics, my first job is to gather all the information and ideas necessary for the designs. I usually do this by going out into the country during all seasons with a sketch book and camera. I draw the individual blooms of flowers from many angles as I want the maximum variety of form in the finished design. Sometimes I see material for a complete design in a section of hedgerow, meadow, or the edge of a field (see figure 11.10). I regard this as a process of observing and absorbing as many varied impressions as possible.

The next stage takes place in my studio, and there, surrounded by my drawings and photographs, I decide how these will be used in the final designs. If it is a collection for dress fabrics, I have to consider the season for which I am designing, and the current 'look' and style that is in demand. When designing furnishing fabrics, wallpaper, and general household linens, the emphasis is more on the particular style of the firm for which I am working.

When working on the designs themselves I have to consider how I can use the materials I have collected, for there are many ways of setting out a design. The motifs can cover the whole fabric area or be arranged in groups, as a plaid, a border (see figure 11.11), or in horizontal or vertical stripes. Other considerations include the number of colours I can use and the fact that it must be technically possible for the design to be printed by the silk-screen method. I usually work in water colour or gouache (an opaque water colour) on sheets of stretched cartridge paper, varying in size according to the individual design.

When a manufacturer buys a design he will often require further modifications or alterations, such as the design being put into repeat according to his specifications. The price I charge often varies according to the complexity of these specifications.

The design is now ready to be handed on to the printers and it is often a year or longer before the finished fabric appears in the shops.

Although there are further stages between the printers and the design appearing on the market (such as advertising) my own involvement finishes with the final sale to the manufacturer. I then return to the countryside seeking inspiration for new designs.

Figure 11.11
The final design.

CHAPTER 12
It's all in the finish

12.1
GREY FABRIC

Even when a fabric has been made by weaving or knitting and possibly already coloured, it cannot be sent direct to the clothing trade. This is because it has not been *finished*, and the finishing may be very important.

Finishing may completely change the aesthetics or performance of the fabric, or both. An old saying in the textile trade is 'the finish makes the fabric'. This is only partly true, because if the basic construction is poor no amount of finishing will make a good fabric from it, but the finish could still make a big difference. All fabrics straight from the loom or knitting machine need some finishing. They need at least one process to make them ready for the clothing trade. Sometimes the fabric is given many processes. Although every additional process costs money, it may be worth while because it will increase the value of the fabric. An unfinished fabric is known as 'grey' or 'greige'.

Figure 12.1 (above)
Tentering machine.

12.2
CLEANING IT UP

The fabric must be cleaned and the most common way to do this is to wash it. In the textile trade the process is usually called *scouring*. The fabric is sometimes washed in what looks like a giant washing machine. More usually it is washed by a continuous process. Sometimes if a very white fabric is wanted, the grey fabric may be bleached before scouring. Bleaching involves the use of chemicals which break down any coloured substances in the fabric.

Q 1
What precautions are likely to be necessary when using bleach?

Q 2
What safety precautions are necessary when using bleach in the home?

A fabric may be 'dry cleaned', but scouring is more usual. Scouring is often called a *routine finish* because it is done to most fabrics.

Another finish is called *tentering* or sometimes *stentering*. Along the edge of a piece of fabric you might see a line of pin marks. When a fabric is finished it may be wrinkled. If there is a pattern it may be distorted, that is, out of shape. It may also be wet. To deal with all these problems, the fabric is held flat on pins or between clips and passed through an oven. For fabrics which can be heat set in this way, this process also fixes the fabric size and prevents shrinkage.

Figure 12.2 (below)
Brushing and steaming machine.

12.3
AESTHETIC CHANGES

Apart from routine finishes, there are special finishes which can alter the aesthetics of a fabric. Most are concerned with appearance and handle. Sometimes a flat, smooth finish is required. One process is *calendering* or pressing. The fabric is passed through heated rollers or flat plates. It is just like pressing with an iron, except it is done continuously and at much greater pressure. Sometimes the surface of the fabric is raised to make it thicker. This gives a very different sort of handle.

Q 3
What other property will be affected by raising the surface?

One method used for raising the surface is brushing, that is, passing the fabric over a stiff brush on a roller. The process is continuous. Flat filament nylon which has been warp-knitted is treated like this. This gives the familiar brushed nylon used for bed linen and nightwear.

EXAMINING WARP-KNIT NYLON AND WARP-KNIT BRUSHED NYLON

YOU WILL NEED:

Sample of warp-knit nylon
Sample of warp-knit brushed nylon

Hand lens

1 Feel the two fabrics.

Q 4
Which feels thicker?

2 Compare the handle of the two fabrics.

Q 5
When you feel the brushed sample, does the fabric appeal to your sense of touch? Why might this be?

3 Using the hand lens, try to observe what happens when the brushed nylon passes over your fingers.

12.4
PERFORMANCE CHANGES

The special finishes which alter the aesthetics of a fabric are usually carried out by mechanical means. They do not involve using chemicals. However, there are other special finishes for fabrics which greatly change the performance. These use chemicals and are sometimes called *functional finishes*.

Q 6
Why is a chemical finish likely to produce greater changes in performance than a physical finish?

IS IT STILL COTTON?

One of the most important chemical finishes changes the properties of cotton. If you recall these (see Chapter 6) you will remember that there are two particular problems. Wrinkle recovery is poor, especially when wet. Also, as cotton is a hydrophilic fibre it does not dry very quickly after washing. Both these properties mean a lot of extra work when textiles made from cotton are washed.

In the 1930s the discovery was made that cotton could be treated with certain chemicals (resins). These properties (poor wrinkle recovery when wet and long drying time) could be completely changed. Treated cotton has a very good wrinkle recovery when washed so it needs very little, if any, ironing. It behaves as a hydrophobic fibre and therefore dries quickly. This discovery was developed to the full commercially after the Second World War.

The 'new' cotton had such uses as shirts, blouses, and sheets. The names used to describe it were the same as those used to describe fabrics made from some of the synthetic fibres because, after all, the properties of good wrinkle recovery and quick drying were the same. So there appeared 'drip-dry', 'minimum iron', and 'easy care' cotton. Now, virtually all cotton fabrics used commercially have a resin treatment. The main exceptions are knitted cotton used for T-shirts, denim and cord jeans, and towels.

Q 7
Why do you think towels are not treated?

COMPARING THE WASHING PERFORMANCE OF PURE COTTON AND RESIN-TREATED COTTON

‖‖‖ **YOU WILL NEED:** ‖‖

Pure cotton fabric, 15-cm square
Resin-treated cotton fabric, 15-cm square

Detergent

Access to washing machine

1 Take both samples of fabric and, using the washing machine, wash them for five minutes at wash code 4 (see table 15.1).

2 Rinse the detergent from the samples.

3 Compare the samples for wrinkle recovery, using the method described in section 7.5.

4 Compare the speed of drying of the samples, using the method described in section 7.6.

Q 8
In your opinion, which of the two fabric samples gives the better performance? Why?

Figure 12.3
'Looks even better on a man.' This advertising slogan for resin-treated cotton has been used for over twenty years.

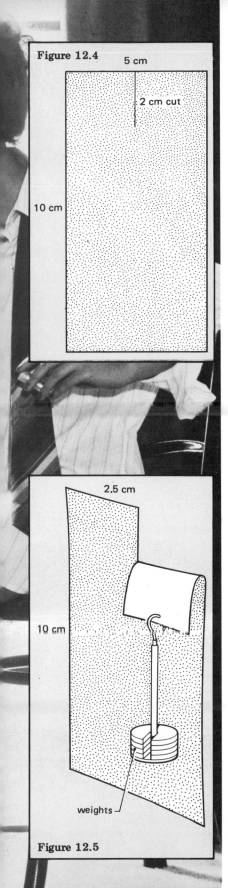

Figure 12.4

Figure 12.5

The treatment carried out on the cotton involves a resin which is a type of polymer. After the processing, the polymer is completely interlinked with the cotton molecules. In places it may be chemically linked to the cotton molecules. This is how it affects the properties of the cotton. The question is: is it still cotton or should it be thought of as a different fibre?

12.5
CHANGES ARE NOT ALWAYS GOOD!

So far, the effect of resin treatment has appeared to be good: improved wrinkle recovery and quick drying. But there is a snag. For reasons which are not entirely understood, the durability of the cotton is greatly reduced. The more resin that is applied, the weaker the fabric becomes, and as much as half the strength may be lost. This is an obvious disadvantage.

COMPARING THE DURABILITY OF PURE COTTON AND RESIN-TREATED COTTON

||| YOU WILL NEED: |||||||||||||||||||||||||||||||||||||||||||||||||||||||||||||||||||||||||||||||||||||||||||||||||||||||||||

Sample of pure cotton	Weights
Sample of resin-treated cotton	Hook
Scissors	Spring balance

1 Measure a strip of fabric 10 cm x 5 cm and cut it out.

2 Make a cut 2 cm long at the centre of the short side of the fabric, as shown in figure 12.4.

3 Hold the fabric on one side of the cut and allow the fabric on the other side to fall forwards.

4 Hang weights on this side of the fabric and continue adding weights until the fabric tears. Figure 12.5 shows this.

5 Note the weight at which this happens.

6 Repeat this with the other fabric sample.

Q 9
Which fabric of the two samples was more durable?

There are also other disadvantages. You saw in Chapter 7 that although a hydrophobic fibre has the advantage of quick drying, it has disadvantages. It does not absorb perspiration easily, and it allows static electricity to build up. This means the fabric will attract dust. Resin-treated cotton is a hydrophobic fibre so it has these disadvantages too. And the application of resin may tend to stiffen the fabrics. This may affect the handle in a way which may not be acceptable. So you see that once again in textiles, nothing happens exactly as you want it to. Resin treatment costs money and may give two very great performance advantages. It can also give at least one performance disadvantage and may affect the aesthetics.

Worksheet FM14 shows you how to treat fabric with resin for yourself and how to test its effects.

12.6
WHAT ABOUT WOOL?

Wool has one very big disadvantage — the problem of shrinkage due to felting (see section 7.5). This, more than anything else, makes wool a problem for those garments which need regular washing. When man-made fibres were introduced, their excellent washing performance gave them a great advantage over wool. Acrylic, in particular, had a handle fairly similar to wool, a reasonable washing performance without shrinking, and was cheaper. This made great inroads into the wool market, particularly in knitwear. For years, scientists have tried to overcome the problem of wool felting, but it is only recently that a really effective treatment has been found.

PUTTING IT RIGHT

Since wool shrinkage results from the wool scales locking into each other, one way of stopping the shrinkage might be to coat the fibre with something which would prevent this movement. This was tried using nylon polymer. The performance was excellent but the aesthetics of wool were lost because the handle, as you would expect, was of nylon.

A simpler treatment was worked out. It was arranged that only a small amount of polymer became attached to the fibre, but still enough to prevent the scales locking. This stopped the shrinkage but at the same time kept the handle of wool. This finish is promoted as 'Superwash'. Apart from costing extra money in processing, it has no disadvantage. However, you might ask 'Is it still wool?' when there is a small amount of another chemical joined to it. Figure 12.6 shows wool fibres treated with resin.

Worksheet FM15 explains what 'Superwash' wool is and suggests an experiment you can carry out for yourself.

12.7
KEEPING OUT THE RAIN

You know that a fabric, woven or knitted, is largely air (see section 7.7). There is air trapped between the fibres in the yarn.

Figure 12.7
Cycling through the monsoon in Rajasthan, India.

Figure 12.8
Traditional riding mac made water-proof with a rubber coating.

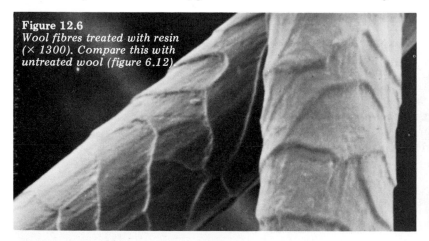

Figure 12.6
Wool fibres treated with resin (× 1300). Compare this with untreated wool (figure 6.12).

In weaving or knitting there are gaps between the yarns, especially in the loops of a knitted structure. No matter how tightly the fabric is made there will always be holes. This is why water will pass through, even if the fibre itself does not absorb water. So, if a garment is worn in the rain it will, in the end, be no protection against it. Yet some countries have a lot of rain.

The obvious way to stop the rain penetrating is to block up the holes in the fabric. This can be done by applying a continuous layer of material on one side. This used to be done with rubber and was the idea behind the original macintosh. Unfortunately, although it kept out the rain it also kept in the perspiration. Because the perspiration cannot evaporate away from the body, it coats the inside of the garment and the wearer becomes more and more uncomfortable. Rubber has now largely been replaced by plastics such as polyurethane, but the problem remains the same. The perspiration stays in if the rain stays out.

IS A COMPROMISE POSSIBLE?

If you put a drop of water on the surface of a fabric it soon soaks in, but fabric can be treated to prevent this. The chemical used to treat fabric is called silicone. This makes the water remain in a drop form and so run easily off the surface.

This treatment with silicone can be done on any reasonably tightly constructed fabric (that is, a fabric where the holes are not too big). The rain is kept out by causing the water to stay in drops and run off. But some holes are still there to allow the perspiration to pass through. It is all a compromise. The holes are still there. If the rain is very heavy it will finally get through. Once again, an extra process costing money has improved the performance. However, neither the continuous coating nor the silicone is entirely satisfactory.

Worksheet FM16 shows you how to test the effectiveness of a commercial water repellent.

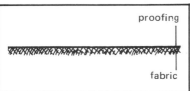

Figure 12.9

Figure 12.10
Most modern anoraks are coated with plastic to keep out the rain and snow

Figure 12.11
A machine which tests waterproof fabric.

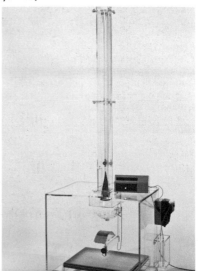

BACKGROUND READING

A PROTECTIVE COAT

Protective clothing comes in all kinds from very simple to very complex, according to the protection needed. Even an ordinary overcoat is protective in a simple way — against cold. A more obvious example is a proofed raincoat. There are many other things against which protection is needed.

In everyday life you may need guarding against the impact of falling off a motorcycle, or the many kinds of heavy blow which you risk in sport. You may need a mask to filter out paint fumes or choking dust, or gloves to protect your hands. If you work in industry you may need protection against heavy objects falling on your head or feet, or corrosive or poisonous chemicals, or the heat of a furnace. Special risks are splashing molten metal in a foundry, or chainsaws in forestry work. Divers need insulation from the icy cold of the ocean. Racing drivers risk both head injuries and fire. Astronauts are exposed to the vacuum of space, and the extremes of the burning heat of the Sun on one side and the sub-zero temperatures of space on the other, as well as micro-meteoroids — tiny particles of rock whizzing through space which can hole a space suit. Soldiers can be partly protected from bullets and shrapnel.

There are several ways of making clothing protective. One is to give fabric a special finish. Waterproofing is the simplest example, but cloth can also be made fire-resistant. The earliest flameproof clothes were made of wool, which is slow to burn, impregnated with borax, a fire-proofing substance. But the powdery borax fell out of the cloth, or came out in the wash, and often had to be renewed. Now there are better treatments, such as the Zirpro process (see figure 12.12). Other fabrics can be made fire-proof too. Cotton can be treated by the Proban process: the finish goes right into the fibre, so it can be washed or dry cleaned. Racing drivers' overalls may be made of Nomex, a modified polyamide fibre. Workers in very hot places have overalls coated with aluminium to reflect heat. Other finishes resist chemicals such as acids.

Another way in which protection is improved is the use of layers. This is an old idea: medieval chainmail had a leather coat underneath to spread the impact of a blow. The padding inside a crash helmet works in the same way. Flameproof overalls are worn over heat-insulating underwear. The impact resistance of a soldier's flak jacket is given by layer upon layer of ultra-strong carbon fibre. The leg-guards a forester wears against chainsaws are made in a similar way. The most layered garment of all is a space suit. The Apollo moonwalkers had an 18-layer suit resisting heat, cold, and micro-meteoroids, worn over a plastic pressure suit and insulating underwear.

Figure 12.12
Testing Zirpro-treated wool.
The man in the first picture can keep his arm in the flames for 20 seconds with only a slight reddening of the skin.
The second picture shows a stunt man trying it out.
(The aircraft seats in figure 11.5 are made of wool which has been Zirpro-treated.)

CHAPTER 13
The garment takes shape

Figure 13.1

13.1
TWO-DIMENSIONAL TO THREE-DIMENSIONAL
The finished fabric is now ready to be made up by the clothing industry. When the fabric leaves the textile mill it may be on a board or a roll. The fabric is a flat two-dimensional material. It must be converted into a three-dimensional garment to provide clothing.

13.2
ENGINEERING THE SHAPE
If two straight fabric edges are joined together, the result is still a flat two-dimensional form, as figure 13.3 shows.

Q 1
Suppose the pieces of fabric being joined together were curved at the edge, what would be the shape when these were joined together? Would the fabric still be two-dimensional?

Different shapes are needed to make fashion styles to fit different parts of the body and to fit different people. A designer is the person who produces patterns to do this. Each pattern is made up of a number of pieces which are joined together in the right order to make the garment (see figure 13.5 on the next page). Each style needs a different pattern. There will be different patterns for the different sizes of the same style. The original style will come from a stylist or designer who specializes in creating new fashions.

Q 2
Can you name a famous fashion designer?

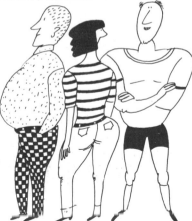

Figure 13.2
Humans are three-dimensional!

Figure 13.3
A flat seam.

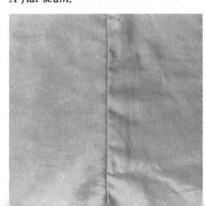

Figure 13.4
Moulded steel: Ford Fiesta production at Dagenham.

ANOTHER WAY

Cutting patterns and engineering different shapes when the pieces are joined together is not the only way of converting a two-dimensional flat fabric into a three-dimensional form. Another way is by moulding, using pressure or heat. An obvious example outside textiles and clothing is the way steel can be moulded into shapes to produce car body panels (see figure 13.4).

In textiles, the ability to mould is limited. However, felt (a non-woven fabric) can be moulded fairly easily. This property can be used to make hats (see figure 13.6 at the top of the next page).

Q 3
Why do you think patterned fabrics would not be moulded?

THE TAILOR'S WAY

Although woven fabrics cannot generally be moulded very much, moulding is a way of getting a three-dimensional shape. The limited ability of textiles to mould is used by tailors to get extra shape and therefore perfect fitting in some garments, particularly jackets. Two pieces of fabric are joined together, with one piece slightly longer than the other. The extra fabric on one side is wrinkled, but when the fabric is pressed with an iron (heat and pressure), this wrinkling is removed as the fabric moulds and therefore a three-dimensional shape is produced. Tailors call this 'putting in fullness'.

HOW IS 'FULLNESS' PUT IN?

‖‖‖ YOU WILL NEED: ‖‖‖

Wool suiting fabric	Scissors
Thread	Needle and pins
	Sewing machine
Iron	
Pressing cloth	

1 Cut one piece of fabric 20 cm x 10 cm, and one piece of fabric 22 cm x 10 cm.

2 Ease stitch along the edge of fabric which measures 22 cm.

Figure 13.5
A fashion drawing. The diagram shows the shapes of the pieces of fabric.

Figure 13.6
Moulding a felt hat.

3 Join the 22-cm length to the 20-cm length, easing the 22-cm length to fit the 20-cm length. Baste.

4 Make a plain open seam with a 1.5-cm seam allowance.

5 Pre-heat the iron at the cotton setting. Damp the pressing cloth. Press the seam open using the damp cloth.

Q 4
What is the shape produced — is it flat or curved?

Q 5
If you were making a jacket, where do you think the join you have just made would be most useful?

You will have found that it was difficult to join fabrics of unequal lengths together, and that it took some care and extra work to press away the fullness and get the desired shape. Therefore, in garment production, those garments where shape is obtained by pressing away the fullness cost more than those where the shape is obtained by simply joining equal lengths of fabric together. This is why a tailored suit is generally expensive.

13.3
JOINING IT UP

Most garments are made by joining differently shaped pieces of fabric together. When so much trouble has been taken to give a fabric the right aesthetics and performance, you would expect that the method of joining would not spoil these in any way. The simplest way to join the fabrics together might be to stick them. So why is it necessary to use a sewing machine and thread to produce complicated stitches?

COMPARING JOINS

‖ **YOU WILL NEED:** ‖‖

Pure cotton fabric	Sewing machine
Thread	Scissors
P.V.A. glue	Glue brush

1 Cut 4 pieces of fabric measuring 20 cm x 10 cm.

Figure 13.7
Tailored jackets are expensive.

2 Take 2 of the fabric pieces and put them with the right sides together.

3 Allowing 1.5 cm for a seam allowance, stitch the fabric pieces together using the sewing machine set on straight stitch (*lock stitch*). Figure 13.8a shows this.

4 Using the two remaining fabric pieces, put them with right sides together.

5 Allowing the same 1.5 cm for a seam allowance, spread the P.V.A. glue along the length of one of the fabric pieces, in the seam allowance (see figure 13.8b).

6 Press the two fabric pieces together and allow the glue to dry.

Q 6
What difference can you see between the two seams you have made?

Q 7
How have the seams affected the handle of the fabric?

Q 8
What effect has the glue had on the performance of the fabric?

Q 9
What effect has the stitched seam had on the performance of the fabric?

Q 10
Which do you think is the better method of joining the pieces of fabric together?

13.4
SEAMS AND PURPOSES
The seam is required to do a number of jobs. As well as retaining the aesthetics, that is the handle and drape of the fabric, it must hold the fabric pieces together at the join so that the garment stays in shape. One of the advantages of sewing as a means of producing a join is that it retains the aesthetics. And different stitches can be made for different types of seams in different fabrics. Three important types of stitch are *lock stitch* (the commonest), *zig-zag stitch*, and *overlock stitch*.

Q 11
One difference between seams is the amount of stretch they allow. Why should this be important?

COMPARING THE STRETCH PROPERTIES OF SEAMS

|||| YOU WILL NEED: ||||||||||||||||||||||||||||||||||||||||||||||||||||||||||||||||||||||||||||
6 pieces of double jersey fabric (each 10 cm X 5 cm)
Cotton thread

Ruler
Sewing machine

1 Take two pieces of the sample fabric and put them right sides together.

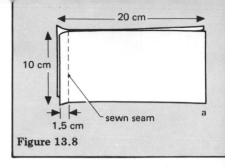

Figure 13.8

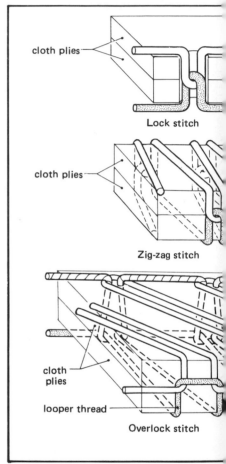

Figure 13.10
Puckered seam.

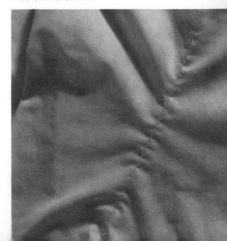

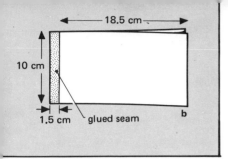

2 Allow 1.5 cm for a seam allowance.

3 Sew a plain open seam using lock stitch.

4 Repeat the process for the remaining two pairs of fabric samples, but for the first pair sew the seam using zig-zag stitch and for the second pair sew the seam using overlock stitch.
(*Note:* Make sure that the same stitch length is used for each seam.)

5 Measure the length of each seam you have sewn.

6 Stretch each seam as far as possible without breaking the stitches. Measure it while stretched.

7 Calculate the percentage stretch of the seam in each case, using the following formula:

$$\frac{\text{stretched length} - \text{original length}}{\text{original length}} \times 100 = \% \text{ stretch}$$

Q 12
Which stitch produced the seam with the greatest percentage stretch?

Q 13
Has the seam with the lowest percentage stretch any advantages over the other two?

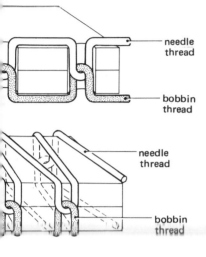

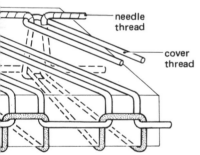

Figure 13.9
Different types of stitching

Figure 13.11
An embarrassing situation.

13.5
GETTING THE RIGHT THREAD
It is important that the performance of the garment is not let down by the sewing thread. If the performance properties of the fabric are not matched by the performance of the sewing thread, this will be a weak link in the garment. The most important properties of a sewing thread are strength and size retention. Size retention for a sewing thread means it must not shrink when it is in the garment. If it did shrink it would make the seam wrinkle. The result would be a poor aesthetic effect. When this happens it is usually called *puckering*. Figure 13.10 shows this.

Strength or durability is, of course, a complicated property (see Chapter 7). If the thread breaks before the garment is worn out then a repair will be necessary. It could be very embarrassing!

A particularly important strain which a sewing thread must bear in a garment is that it must be able to stretch and recover from that stretch. In particular, it must be able to stretch as much as the fabric in which it is being used. Some fabrics stretch more than others.

Q 14
Which method of construction gives fabrics the greatest stretch?

You have seen that certain seams using certain stitches stretch more than others. Sometimes, particularly when a lock stitch is used, the stretch must come from the thread itself. If the fabric cannot stretch at the seam because the thread is holding it back, the thread may break.

The traditional sewing thread is cotton. However, it has several disadvantages. Firstly, although quite strong, it is rotted by perspiration. In certain seams, such as under the arms, it can break down quite quickly. Secondly, it tends to shrink when wet, so seams made from it may pucker. Thirdly, it has low stretch. In recent years polyester has been used more and more for sewing threads. It is much stronger and much more resistant to perspiration. It does not shrink when wet and has much more stretch.

Sewing threads are sold in different thicknesses. The thickness is described by a *count* or number. The thicker the thread the stronger it will be. However, a cotton thread has to be thicker than a polyester thread to give the same strength. A thick thread will not give such a neat seam.

COMPARING THE STRETCH PROPERTIES OF SEAMS USING DIFFERENT THREADS

|||| YOU WILL NEED: |||||||||||||||||||||||||||||||||||||||||||||||||||||||||||||||||||||||||||||||||||||||||

4 pieces of double jersey fabric (each 10 cm × 5 cm)
Cotton thread
Polyester thread of similar size

Ruler
Sewing machine

1 Take two pieces of the fabric and place them right sides together. Allow 1.5 cm for a seam allowance.

2 Thread up the sewing machine using the cotton thread. Sew a plain open seam using lock stitch.

3 Repeat the above process, but this time sew the remaining two pieces of fabric together using polyester thread.

4 Measure the length of the cotton seam. Measure the length of the polyester seam.

5 Stretch the seams as far as possible without breaking the thread, and remeasure them while stretched.

6 Calculate the percentage stretch of the seam, using the formula given in section 13.4.

Q 15
Which sewing thread gives the largest percentage stretch in a seam?

Figure 13.14
Apparatus to measure the temperature at the eye of a needle during sewing.

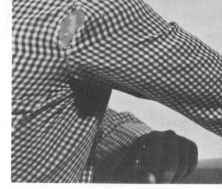

Figure 13.12
The cotton thread broke in the seam.

Polyester filament sewing thread

polyester filaments

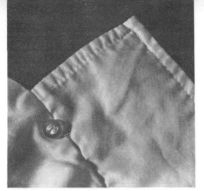

Figure 13.13
The cotton thread and the interlining shrank.

ore spun polyester/cotton sewing thread

olyester
laments

cotton
fibres

COTTON WINS THE SECOND ROUND

When polyester has such superior properties to cotton in a sewing thread, you may wonder why cotton is used at all. So far, only performance in the seam has been considered, but performance in sewing must be considered as well. During sewing, the top thread passes through the eye of the needle. This moves in and out of the fabric. As the needle passes through the fabric it becomes hot due to *friction*. The faster the machine sews (and industrial sewing machines sew as many as 7000 stitches per minute) the more heating occurs.

Q 16
What else is likely to affect the amount of heat produced?

The temperature around the eye of the needle can reach well over 200 °C. Polyester melts at approximately 220 °C! So polyester threads may break down during sewing. Cotton can withstand higher temperatures, so *needle heat* is less of a problem. See figures 13.14 and 13.16 (below left and below right).

COMPROMISE AGAIN

The original polyester threads were made from filament polyester yarn. Whilst having excellent properties in the seam, they caused great problems during sewing with fast industrial machines. A compromise was worked out between cotton, which worked well in the sewing machine but had relatively poor performance properties, and polyester, which sewed badly but had good performance. Cotton was spun around the outside of a polyester filament. This gave a *core spun polyester/cotton sewing thread* (see figure 13.15).

As the sewing thread passes through the needle, the cotton covering protects the polyester from needle heat. The performance of the polyester core gives the required properties in the seam.

Figure 13.15 (left)
a *Photograph of thread with polyester core and cotton wrapping (× 300).*
b *Sewing threads in cross-section.*

Figure 13.16 (below)
Fabric sewability tester. This measures the force required for a needle to penetrate the fabric. The greater the force the more likely it is that sewing will damage the fabric.

Another method which has been successful in overcoming the problem of needle heat is to use yarn spun from polyester staple fibre. The reason why this works is that the air trapped around the bulky staple yarn acts as an insulator. This slows down the conduction of heat from the needle to the thread (see Chapter 7) and allows the thread to pass through the needle without damage (see figure 13.17). Compare this with the smooth flat filament yarn which rubs against the inside of the needle eye. Remember that cotton thread is spun from staple fibre.

Most of the polyester threads now on the market are either core spun polyester/cotton or 100 per cent polyester spun from staple fibre.

13.6
OTHER TRIMMINGS
In Chapter 2 you found that apart from threads there were a number of other trimmings in a garment. The performance of the trimming must also be the same as the performance of the main fabric. Each trimming may have certain properties which are more important than others. For instance, an interlining is put in a garment to change the handle at a particular point, perhaps to make the front of a jacket stiffer and help it keep its shape. Clearly, an interlining must have good wrinkle recovery. And if the lining of a washable garment were to shrink during washing it could badly distort the shape of the garment.

Q 17
List the properties you think are important in the following trimmings:
a. suit jacket lining
b the tape of a zip
c shirt collar interlining.

Once again, the trimmings have to be assessed in terms of the three factors: aesthetics, performance, and price. These factors must always be related to the main fabric.

BACKGROUND READING

THE FASHION DESIGNER
The clothes you buy and wear have been designed by someone for your needs. This is so whether the garment is a new dress or shirt for a party or even a school uniform.

What do you think fashion is? One year often has quite a different 'feel' from another. Sometimes fashion designers can change the shape and direction of fashion throughout the World. If they are on the right 'wave length' their designs will be taken up and developed by other clothing designers for mass markets. Examples are the 'New Look' produced by Dior after the Second World War and the mini-skirt of the 1960s. Many fashion

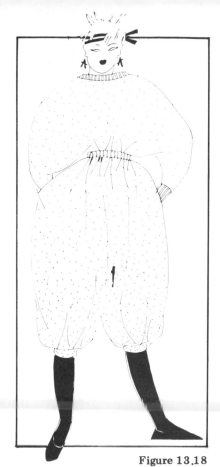

Figure 13.18

designers work for large clothing manufacturers, adapting the ideas that are around to the needs of their companies and their customers, that is, you.

All these designers have to have an imaginative flair for being sensitive to what people will want to look like in a year's time. Some ideas do come from top fashion designers, but there are other influences as well. Styles may be revived or introduced by a popular television series or film. The Princess of Wales is tall and caused a fashion for flat-heeled shoes. We are very conscious of how people in other parts of the World dress; Indian clothes and American baseball shirts are often in and out of fashion. 'Anti-fashion' such as punk becomes fashion. Training shoes are worn by many people who don't go running!

The designer must think of the fabric as well as the shape of the finished garment. Of course, fashion designers are limited by what it is possible for manufacturers to produce as well as what people want. Their companies have to compete with each other and with goods which sell because they are cheap. Most clothes now have to be designed for mass production. For instance, a fancy collar might be too expensive — or impossible — if the machine available could not produce it. The designer might be told that the manufacturer did not want to have a pocket on each side of a shirt because of the difficulty of getting them exactly on the same level. To reduce costs the range of different designs available may be reduced in size and scope so that there are fewer designs to choose from. There will always be a demand for unusual garments from some people, but as these clothes will be much more difficult to make they will obviously be more expensive.

Most people today want clothes that are comfortable to wear and easy to take care of. A garment must be very special if it can't be washed or at least dry cleaned. Most designers would agree with the successful American designer, Calvin Klein, who says that he produces 'clothes for the life we live'. Practical clothes do not have to be dull or uninteresting.

Designers today must know about new fabrics, mass production techniques, and what the buyers will want. They must be versatile and adaptable to vary their approach depending on the company and the market they are working for, and must develop a strong creative professional approach.

Figure 13.17

CHAPTER 14
Getting dirty

14.1
LIVING IN DIRT

You have bought a garment and will very quickly find out if the performance properties built into it meet the requirements of living. The garment will undoubtedly get dirty and need cleaning. Clothes get dirty even in a house which is cleaned thoroughly every day because you live in a cloud of dust. Have you ever looked at a beam of sunlight shining through a window? If so, you will have seen that the air is full of tiny particles all moving about. These particles are visible because they are reflecting the sunlight, but they are still there even when the sunlight has gone. The whole atmosphere is full of dust. Whatever you do, you are living in a cloud of dust.

This dust is not only in the air; it is also on the ground, on the furniture, in fact on everything. The dust comes from a whole variety of sources. Here are some examples.
All animals, including humans, are constantly shedding dead skin particles which become part of the dust.
Textiles and other materials wear away, and the debris becomes part of the dust.
Trees and plants shed small seeds, pollen, and so on. When the trees and plants die they crumble to dust.
So the supply of dust never ends.

Figure 14.1
Shafts of light show up because of dust in the air. ('The creation of light' by Gustave Doré.)

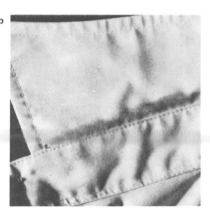

Figure 14.2
a *Fibres in a soiled polyester/cotton shirt collar (× 700).*
b *The shirt collar.*

Figure 14.3

Q 1
If there is a never-ending supply of dust, why is the World not knee-deep in dust?

Some of the dust will become attached to you and your clothing. How does it do this? This can happen by simple physical means; it becomes entangled or trapped in the uneven surface of the clothes.

EXAMINING DUST CLINGING TO A FABRIC

|||| YOU WILL NEED: ||||||||||||||||||||||||||||||||||||||||||||||||||||||||||||||||||||||||||||||||||||||||||
Sample of fabric which has recently been laundered
Small amount of dust

Hand lens

1 Take the clean fabric and examine the surface using the hand lens.

2 Shake some dust onto the fabric.

3 Shake off the excess dust.

4 Observe the fabric again using the hand lens.

5 Write down the differences you can see this time.

14.2
REMOVING THE DUST
Dust is everywhere and cannot be avoided, but if it is only attached by simple physical means it should be very easy to remove. When a duster is shaken, most of the dust comes off.

Q 2
Suggest two other ways dirt could be removed.

Unfortunately there is an additional factor. There is another source of dirt or soil which causes the dust to become attached more securely to the clothes. This is grease or oil.

14.3
GREASE FROM WITHIN AND WITHOUT
Everyone knows that clothes get dirty when they come into contact with oil or grease.

Unless you work somewhere like a garage, this soiling only happens in large amounts occasionally. There is another source of oil or grease which is there all the time. Perspiration from the body carries with it oils and greases, and so clothes gradually get soiled from within. Some people produce more grease in their skins than others and are said to have a greasy skin. Ordinary dust from outside sticks to the grease. An obvious place where this happens is on a shirt or blouse collar, where the fabric is not only in contact with the skin, but also exposed to the dust outside. (See figure 14.2 above.)

So cleaning is not as simple as removing dust. The real problem is removing grease or oil.

14.4
HOW DIRTY CAN YOU GET?
You can get very dirty and some people are very good at it.

In everyday wear, some fabrics become dirty more easily than others. A fabric with a smooth surface is likely to stay cleaner than one with a rough surface.

Q 3

Why do you think this is so?

Q 4

What common household article has its surface deliberately roughened?

Remember the effect of static electricity (see Chapter 7). You could investigate this using worksheet FM17.

Q 5

Which fabrics are likely to become most dirty due to static electricity?

Finally, some fabrics may show dirt more easily than others although they might not be more dirty.

Q 6

What fabrics are likely to show dirt more than others?

You can learn more about soiling and cleaning in *People and homes* Chapter 5.

Figure 14.4

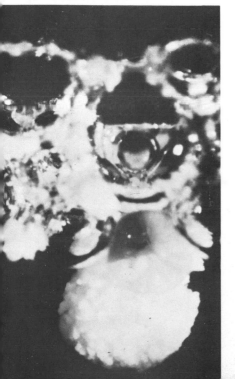

Figure 14.5
Clear bubbles of detergent carrying small globules of fat.

BACKGROUND READING

THE LONG FIGHT AGAINST DIRT

Ever since fabrics were invented they have been getting dirty. For most of this time — and certainly in all civilized societies — people have been trying to clean them by various methods. Through the ages the nature of the dirt has changed. On the whole it has become greasier and blacker, and harder to remove. Each new invention — the oil lamp, the candle, coal burning, oily machinery, the car, and tough modern paints and adhesives — has brought new and thorny problems of soiling. In turn, better cleaning methods have been devised.

For a long time washing was the only way of cleaning fabrics. There were some simple substances to help. Some plants have roots which yield a soapy stuff, saponin, which froths in water and washes quite well. One of these plants found in Britain is soapwort, a wild relative of the carnation. There are many others. Less pleasant but quite effective is cow's urine, which has a bleaching effect. Of course it has to be well rinsed out afterwards.

The ancient Greeks and Romans used to rub themselves with olive oil as a skin tonic. It must have made a mess of their clothes. Statues of Romans show them wearing a toga. This was a wraparound woollen garment which had to be white, by law. Only senators and other important people could wear togas with purple edges. The toga trailed on the ground and got badly soiled. The Romans hated wearing it, and only put it on for formal occasions. At other times they wore simple robes of Greek design, in dark colours which did not show the dirt. By this time soap had been developed. At first it was made by boiling a mixture of fat and the ash of some plants which contain soda.

The elaborate robes worn by the rich in the Middle Ages were made of heavy fabrics which were hard to clean. Washing made the fabric go out of shape. The only successful method was to take the garment completely apart, wash it, and sew it back together again. Light cleaning could be done with fuller's earth, a dry, grease-absorbing powder. (Modern 'dry shampoo' is fuller's earth.)

In the nineteenth century the sooty coal fires and factory chimneys of the towns made clothes and furnishings filthy. To everyone's relief dry cleaning was invented in 1825 when a Frenchman, Jean-Baptiste Jolly, spilt paraffin on a tablecloth and noticed how it dissolved greasy dirt. From the 1850s, better, factory-made soap was widely sold. By 1900 one could buy both fine toilet soap and the first soap flakes and powders specially for washing fabrics. Even these did not work well in hard water, forming a nasty scum. In the past thirty years synthetic detergents, which do not have that drawback, have largely taken over.

CHAPTER 15
Keep it clean

15.1
DISSOLVING OUT THE GREASE

If grease or oil is the main cause of soiling, either alone or because dust is sticking to it, an obvious way to clean it off is to use something which dissolves the grease. If the grease is removed then the dust might go with it. This is the idea behind so-called 'dry cleaning'. Really the word 'dry' is not correct but the idea comes from the fact that the grease is dissolved in a solvent which is not water. The main solvent used now is called perchloroethylene but this is gradually being replaced by trichlorotrifluoroethane (known as Solvent 113). Dry cleaning can be effective but it needs expensive equipment not really practical in the home. Therefore dry cleaning is carried out in special shops and is an expensive way of cleaning clothes.

15.2
WATER: CHEAP BUT INEFFICIENT

Water is cheap and easily available but it will not dissolve grease or oil by itself. If you have ever tried to wash greasy hands with water alone you will know what happens. The water does not cut through the grease but remains on the surface as drops. (See figure 15.2.)

15.3
MAKING WATER WORK

When a drop of water is put on a fabric it stays on the surface and will not immediately sink in, that is, it will not wet the fabric. This is because of *surface tension* (see worksheet FM18).

A detergent will get between the water molecules and break down the surface tension. The water can then wet the fabric and be able to remove some of the dirt. (See figure 15.3.)

Although water can remove some dirt, it cannot remove greasy dirt on its own. Here the detergent has another part to play.

Figure 15.1
Dry cleaning shop.

Figure 15.2

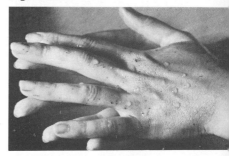

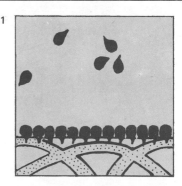

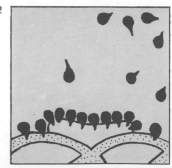

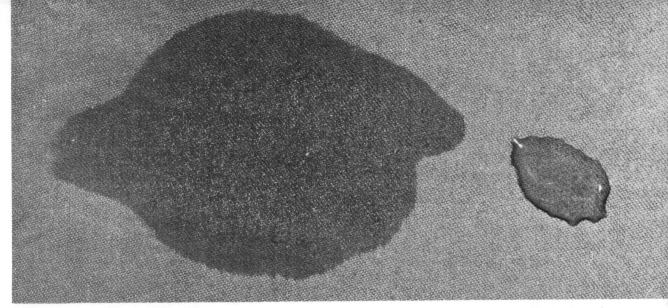

Figure 15.3 (above)
(right) Drop of water on fabric.
(left) The effect of adding detergent.

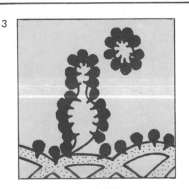

hydrocarbon tail
(hydrophobic)

hydrophilic
group

Figure 15.4
Detergent molecule.

Figure 15.5 (below)
*The way in which a detergent
removes grease from a fibre.*

3

4

Detergents are chemicals containing a long chain of carbon and hydrogen atoms (a *hydrocarbon tail*). At the other end of the chain is a group of atoms which is soluble in water. Therefore a detergent consists of a tail which is hydrophobic (water hating) and a head which is hydrophilic (water loving).

WASHING WITH AND WITHOUT DETERGENT

|||| YOU WILL NEED: ||||||||||||||||||||||||||||||||||||||||||||||||||||||||||||||||||||||||||||||||||
Cotton fabric (2 pieces)   Detergent
Sewing machine oil   Stopwatch or clock
Water as hot as the hand can
comfortably withstand

1 Take the two cotton samples and put a few drops of sewing machine oil on each piece. Allow to soak in.

2 Wash one cotton piece in water alone. Have the water as hot as your hand can comfortably bear.

3 Wash the second cotton piece in water with detergent. (Remember to wash each piece for exactly the same amount of time.)

4 Rinse in lukewarm water.

5 Dry the cotton samples.

6 Compare the results.

Q 1
Which fabric sample is cleaner?

Detergents remove greasy dirt because the hydrophobic tails of the molecule are attracted to the grease and form a layer over the surface. The grease rolls up into drops coated with detergent molecules which are removed from the fabric by agitation. This can be done by hand, by boiling, or by a washing machine. Figure 15.5 shows this.

105

15.4
SOAP OR DETERGENT?

You may have noticed that in the last section only the word detergent was used. There was no mention of soap. Detergent means 'a substance which helps to remove dirt'. By this definition, soap is also a detergent. Products commonly called detergents should really be called soapless or synthetic detergents.

Soaps and synthetic detergents can both be effective cleaners, but something in the water can make soaps less effective than synthetic detergents.

15.5
WHAT IS IN WATER?

To understand what is in the water you must think of rain falling on the hills and collecting in lakes or reservoirs. As the water passes over the rocks and earth into the reservoirs, it will pick up impurities.

Figure 15.6
Cow Green reservoir.

These impurities can be dirt of various sorts, germs, or salts and other chemical compounds which have dissolved in the water from the rocks. The water stands in the reservoir and then has to be treated at the waterworks before it can be used. It is filtered through beds of sand and gravel. This removes the dirt and rubbish. It may be treated with chemicals (chlorinated) to kill off germs. The water is then fit for drinking, but the dissolved salts remain.

Q 2
How could the dissolved salts be removed? Why is this not done?

Some of the salts contained in the water are salts of calcium and magnesium. These cause water hardness. The amount of these salts present in the water depends on where you live. The worst areas are those where the water is collected in limestone or chalk (calcium carbonate). The area around London is like this.

There are two forms of water hardness: *temporary hardness* which can be removed by boiling, and *permanent hardness* which cannot.

HOW HARD IS THE WATER?

 YOU WILL NEED:

Distilled water	3 boiling-tubes and corks
Tap water	Dropper
Hard water	Measuring cylinder
Soap solution	Stopwatch or clock

1 Fill a boiling-tube with 20 ml distilled water and add 2 or 3 drops of soap solution. Cork the tube and shake it for 5 seconds. Note what happens.

2 Repeat the above using hard water, but this time continue to add the soap 2 or 3 drops at a time until a lather is obtained which lasts for a minute. Record the number of drops added.

Figure 15.7
Micro-strainer in waterworks.

3 Repeat this using the tap water, again adding the soap solution until a lather which lasts for a minute is obtained. Again record the number of drops added.

Q 3
Is the tap water hard or soft?

HARD ON SOAP . . .
Hard water will not lather easily with soap. The dissolved calcium and magnesium salts react with the soap to give a scum which will not dissolve. Some of the soap is used up and the scum can be deposited on clothes. Hard water therefore wastes soap, and so soap is not as effective in hard water areas.

NOT SO HARD ON DETERGENTS
Synthetic or soapless detergents do not react with calcium and magnesium salts dissolved in the water, and therefore are not affected by hard water. So in hard water areas it is better to use synthetic detergents.

WATER SOFTENERS
Hard water is a problem when washing and also causes problems in water systems, so many methods have been devised to soften it.

Certain chemical compounds are known which combine with the calcium salts in the water and prevent them from forming compounds with soap. These substances are called *water softeners*. Bath salts are water softeners which have been perfumed. To make things easier, water softeners are often added to soap powders so that the water is softened at the time the soap is added. This leads to a more efficient wash.

WHAT IS THE EFFECT OF A WATER SOFTENER?

IIII YOU WILL NEED: IIIIIIIIIIIIIIIIIIIIIIIIIIIIIIIIIIIIIIIIIIIIIIIIIIIIIIIIIIIIIIIIIIIIIIIIIIIIIIIIIIIIIIIIIIIIIIII
Hard water sample   Boiling-tubes and dropper
Soap solution   Measuring cylinder
Water softener   Stopwatch or clock

1 Fill a boiling-tube with 20 ml hard water.

2 Add 2 or 3 drops of soap solution and shake it for 5 seconds. Continue to add the soap solution 2 or 3 drops at a time, until a lather which lasts for a minute is obtained.

3 Record how many drops of soap solution were required to form the lather.

4 Repeat the experiment, but add a pinch of water softener to the water.

5 Record the amount of soap solution needed the second time.

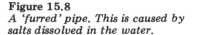

Figure 15.8
A 'furred' pipe. This is caused by salts dissolved in the water.

Q 4
Does the water softener make a difference?

15.6
GETTING IT CLEAN

You can now see what are needed for effective cleaning: water and detergent. Whilst water and detergent will work in the cold (and in some European countries and the United States cold water detergents are used), most detergents work best at a higher temperature — the higher the better.

Q 5

What is the highest temperature that could be obtained under normal conditions using water?

Another important thing is some means of stirring or *agitation*. This helps to remove dirt from the surface of the fabric. After washing, the clothes must be rinsed. Rinsing is the means whereby the dirty water is removed. Several rinses may be necessary.

WASHING EQUIPMENT

The final thing needed for effective washing is a container. The simplest form of washing is hand washing. The container is a bowl or sink, and the agitation is provided by the hands. The maximum temperature possible is 50 °C which is what most hands can bear without protection. Even this may be too hot for some people.

Years ago the main method of washing was a 'copper'. Some are still used today.

Figure 15.9
Hand washing in Britain today and in nineteenth-century Alsace.

Figure 15.10
A 'copper' was used for boiling clothes.

In this method, the 'copper' is filled from the top and the water is heated by solid fuel, gas, or electricity. The temperature is difficult to control using this method. The agitation is achieved either by the movement of the water when boiling or by using a stick. Nowadays, most washing is carried out in a washing machine. The earliest machines were simply electrically heated boilers with a pump for filling and emptying water. Now washing machines have a means of agitating the wash. There are several methods used to cause agitation.(See figures 15.11, 15.12, and 15.13 on the opposite page.)

Washing machines also have means of controlling the temperature of the wash and the filling and emptying of water. Automatic machines have a series of controlled rinses. In addition, there may be a spin programme and even a tumble dry sequence. With all this equipment it should be easy to put the clothes in the machine, add the detergent, heat the water to a high temperature (even boiling), give the maximum agitation for a good length of time, and take out a perfectly clean garment. But there are problems. These are concerned with the performance properties of the fibres and fabrics.

15.7
BUT IT WON'T WORK FOR EVERYTHING

The ideal washing conditions just would not be suitable for every fabric. Some fabrics are too weak to be so roughly treated.

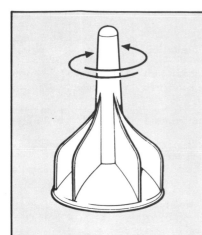
Figure 15.11
The paddle is a fin-shaped spindle which moves backwards and forwards.

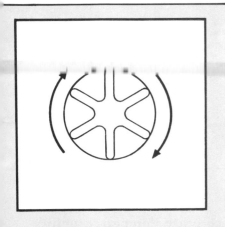
Figure 15.12
The impeller is a rotating wheel on the side or back of the washer.

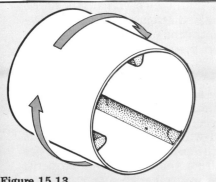
Figure 15.13
The tumbler: here the whole wash drum rotates. This is used in most automatic washing machines.

In some fabrics, the dyes may not be fast to washing at high temperatures. Other fabrics would crease badly at high temperatures and then need ironing, but crease very little at lower temperatures.

COMPARING THE EFFECT OF DIFFERENT WASHING METHODS ON POLYESTER FABRIC

IIII YOU WILL NEED: IIIIIIIIIIIIIIIIIIIIIIIIIIIIIIIIIIIIIIIIIIIIIIIIIIIIIIIIIIIIIIIIIIIIIIIIIIIIIIIIIIIIIIIIIIIIIII

2 pieces of polyester fabric	Saucepan
(30 cm × 30 cm)	Bowl
Detergent	Washing tongs
	Rubber gloves
	Access to cooker

1 Take one piece of fabric and wash it carefully by hand, in hand hot water, using a little detergent. Rinse it with cold water, adding the water to the bowl containing the washing water until the detergent is rinsed out. Remove it from the water and hang it up to drip dry.

2 Take the other piece of fabric and put it in the saucepan. Add detergent and water. Put it on the cooker and bring the water to the boil. Agitate the fabric from time to time with the washing tongs. Boil it for 5 minutes. Remove it from the saucepan with the tongs. Wearing the rubber gloves, wring the fabric. Rinse it in hot water and wring it again. Hang it up to drip dry.

3 Compare the appearance of the two fabric samples when dry.

Q 6
What property of the polyester fabric is affecting its appearance after washing in both cases?

Once again in textiles a compromise is needed, or more precisely a series of compromises. The ideal conditions for washing are not always ideal for the fabrics. To get the best fabric performance a different set of washing conditions may be needed.

15.8
GETTING IT RIGHT IN PRACTICE
As new man-made fibres came onto the market, people did not know how to wash them. At one time, garments and textiles tended to have different washing instructions depending on who wrote the label. This made the job of cleaning textiles difficult, because faced with a load of washing no-one wants to wash each garment separately. To simplify the problem, all the industries with an interest in textile care labelling came together at the Home Laundering Consultative Council (H.L.C.C.) to devise a system of labelling. This was introduced in the United Kingdom in 1965. It arranged textiles into distinct groups for cleaning purposes. Each group was given a number. In 1973 the labels were revised slightly: the washing temperature was put in the washtub symbol, and bleaching, ironing, and dry cleaning instructions were also added. The same system is still used in

Table 15.1
Summary of washing symbols and processes.

Symbol	Washing temperature		Agitation	Rinse	Spinning/wringing
	Machine	Hand			
1 / 95	very hot 95 °C to boil	hand-hot 50 °C or boil	maximum	normal	normal
2 / 60	hot 60 °C	hand-hot 50 °C	maximum	normal	normal
3 / 60	hot 60 °C	hand-hot 50 °C	medium	cold	short spin or drip dry
4 / 50	hand-hot 50 °C	hand-hot 50 °C	medium	cold	short spin or drip dry
5 / 40	warm 40 °C	warm 40 °C	maximum	normal	normal
6 / 40	warm 40 °C	warm 40 °C	minimum	cold	short spin
7 / 40	warm 40 °C	warm 40 °C	minimum do not rub	normal	normal spin do not hand wring
8 / 30	cool 30 °C	cool 30 °C	minimum	cold	short spin do not hand wring
9 / 95	very hot 95 °C to boil	hand-hot 50 °C or boil	medium	cold	drip dry

	DO NOT MACHINE WASH
	DO NOT WASH

the United Kingdom and in some other European countries. The washing instructions are printed on labels which are sewn into garments. Figure 7.18 on page 56 shows some examples.

The washing processes used in each case are those which take into account the fabric properties and give, on balance, the best washing conditions. The aim is that garments which have been cleaned under the correct conditions retain their aesthetic characteristics, even if sometimes they need to be ironed to remove wrinkles.

In this way garments come to the end of the chain. They have been selected by the consumer on the basis of aesthetics, performance, and price. Having been worn, they can be serviced at the minimum possible cost and worn again. Since nothing is perfect and nothing lasts for ever, the considerations of aesthetics and performance will change during the life of the garment. Fashions may change so that it is no longer so attractive. The colour may fade or it may wear into a hole. The consumer will then judge whether he or she has had value for money and, with this in mind, go out and buy another garment.

Fabric	Benefits
White cotton and linen articles without special finishes	Ensures whiteness and stain removal
Cotton, linen, or viscose articles without special finishes where colours are fast at 60 °C	Maintains colours
White nylon; white polyester/cotton mixtures	Prolongs whiteness — minimizes creasing
Coloured nylon; polyester; cotton and viscose articles with special finishes; acrylic/cotton mixtures; coloured polyester/cotton mixtures	Safeguards colour and finish — minimizes creasing
Cotton, linen, or viscose articles where colours are fast at 40 °C, but not at 60 °C	Safeguards the colour fastness
Acrylics; acetate and triacetate, including mixtures with wool; polyester/wool blends	Preserves colour and shape — minimizes creasing
Wool, including blankets, and wool mixtures with cotton or viscose; silk	Keeps colour, size, and handle
Silk and printed acetate fabrics with colours not fast at 40 °C	Prevents colour loss
Cotton articles with special finishes capable of being boiled but requiring drip drying	Prolongs whiteness, retains special crease-resistant finish

WASHING TEMPERATURES

100 °C **Boil**
Self-explanatory.

95 °C **Very hot**
Water heated to near boiling temperature.

60 °C **Hot**
Hotter than the hand can bear. The temperature of water coming from many domestic hot taps.

50 °C **Hand-hot**
As hot as the hand can bear.

40 °C **Warm**
Pleasantly warm to the hand.

30 °C **Cool**
Cool to the touch.

BACKGROUND READING

THE WORLD OF DETERGENTS

Detergents are simple products, you might think, and not very exciting. Yet they are given a fierce 'hard-sell' treatment, with long, dramatic, and expensive television commercials. This is all the more surprising when you read the small print on the side of the packet and discover that all the brands are made by half a dozen large companies. Any one company markets several brands which compete with each other.

The effect of all this campaigning is to make people buy more detergents and more advanced kinds — which means more expensive ones. This is profitable for the companies, but also for the public. Under all the hype, serious research is being done and detergents are really getting better.

Detergent companies usually make all kinds of other cleaners and toiletries, and often other products such as drugs or plastics. They have large departments concerned with new products. The actual scientific work of devising better detergents and new additives is done in the Development department. For example, technologists discovered in the 1960s that if small amounts of digestive enzymes, as used by animals to digest food, were added to detergent they would 'eat' biological stains.

Another department is Product Appraisal. Here they assess what the buyer needs or wants. They send researchers into people's homes to offer samples of new products for trial, and to find out how people wash their clothes, how much powder they use, or whether they bother to read the instructions. For example, the new enzyme detergents only worked properly if clothes were soaked before washing. Many people did not realize this and were disappointed at the results.

Another department called Quality Control investigates complaints about products which are not performing well. Trouble may be caused by misuse, such as not soaking. Or there may be something really wrong. With the early biological detergents there were complaints that the enzymes caused skin rashes. The problem was thrown back at Development, who devised different additives which did as good a job with no harmful effects.

The advertising agency which produces the commercials is a separate firm. The copywriters and artists here have the tricky job of creating advertisements which at the same time please the detergent firm's executives and actually make the public buy the goods. Also, they have to keep their claims within the strict rules of truthfulness laid down by the Advertising Standards Authority.

Figure 15.14
Detergents are sold very forcefully all over the World. This mobile demonstration is in Zimbabwe.

Index